Advance Praise

"With warmth and humility, Daniela Gitlin's new book eluci-
dates the importance of 'doorknob bombshells'—those highly
significant, last-minute revelations familiar to clinicians of
all stripes—and the rationale for respecting them by holding
fast to the therapeutic frame. Deftly integrating neurobiology
and attachment theory, Gitlin draws on her experiences as
both a psychiatrist and a writer to show how the process of
therapy parallels the creative process, and the potential for
doorknob moments to promote trust and growth in the therapeutic relationship."

—**Karen Perlman, PhD,** LP, NCPsyA

"The last minutes of a therapy session may pose such challenges as an 'exit line' or 'curtain call'; the patient delivers
a parting shot that either forces an extension of the time or
lingers as a message until the next appointment. Dr. Gitlin's
thoughtful and scholarly book focuses on the moment when
a patient, one hand often literally on the doorknob, drops a
'bombshell,' ranging from a startling insight to a scary crisis."

—**Alvin Pam, PhD,** clinical psychologist

"*Doorknob Bombshells in Therapy* is an in-depth exploration
of the complicated and powerful relationship between a
patient and a therapist. By exploring the moment that leads
to the end of a therapy session, Dr. Gitlin provides insight in
the entire meaning of the therapeutic alliance that is built."

—**Jeffrey Stovall, MD,** professor of clinical psychiatry,
department of psychiatry and behavioral sciences,
Vanderbilt University Medical Center

T0205083

DOORKNOB BOMBSHELLS IN THERAPY

ALSO BY DANIELA V. GITLIN, MD

Practice, Practice, Practice: This Psychiatrist's Life

DOORKNOB BOMBSHELLS IN THERAPY

*The Deadline, the Brain,
and Why It Is Important
to End on Time*

Daniela V. Gitlin, MD

Norton Professional Books
*An Imprint of W. W. Norton & Company
Independent Publishers Since 1923*

Copyright © 2024 by Daniela V. Gitlin

For information about permission to reproduce selections from this book, write to Permissions, W. W. Norton & Company, Inc., 500 Fifth Avenue, New York, NY 10110

For information about special discounts for bulk purchases, please contact W. W. Norton Special Sales at specialsales@wwnorton.com or 800-233-4830

Manufacturing by Versa Press
Production manager: Gwen Cullen

ISBN: 978-1-324-05259-3 (pbk)

W. W. Norton & Company, Inc., 500 Fifth Avenue, New York, NY 10110
www.wwnorton.com

W. W. Norton & Company Ltd., 15 Carlisle Street, London W1D 3BS

1 2 3 4 5 6 7 8 9 0

For my patients,
in gratitude for showing me the way.

For my colleagues,
in hopes this will make your working life easier.

CONTENTS

It's still magic even if you know how it's done.

— TERRY PRATCHETT, *A Hat Full of Sky*

INTRODUCTION

> The clock has run out on my session with Sarah. I've
> got my hand on the doorknob, ready to walk her
> out—and that's when she tells me she was sexually
> molested by her mother's boyfriend when she was
> eight, and breaks down, weeping wretchedly.

We've all had this experience of patients dropping a
shocker—a critical disclosure that moves the treatment
forward—on their way out the door. This therapeutic
phenomenon, known as the *doorknob moment*, occurs
all too often and never predictably. When a patient
sobs heartbrokenly following a last-minute revelation,
it feels at least unkind and at worst harmful to say,
"Sorry, too bad you're bleeding, we don't have time to
pack that wound."

I was taught as a resident that it is therapeutic to
end as scheduled, *but not why*. As a caring clinician, not
having a sound therapeutic reason to end on time has
required me to make a case-by-case, on-the-spot judgment call: whether to process the material with the
patient right then and run over or to end on time with

a promise that we'll start the next session with what the patient just revealed.

Running late derails the day's schedule (stressful for us) and inconveniences subsequent patients (stressful for them, and possibly undermining to their treatments). I know a last-minute bombshell will drop, but not when, how, or who will drop it. And when it hits, having to make that judgment call in seconds, for me, has been an ongoing source of professional stress for almost three decades.

Until . . . the formulation I present in this book came to me in an electrifying flash, fully formed, and three-dimensional—*Eureka! I have it!* I felt like Archimedes must have, leaping from his bath full of joy that the solution to the riddle of buoyancy had come to him. At the time I was sitting at my desk working on my first book, and I jumped up from my chair to do a happy dance. Yes, it *is* therapeutic to end on time!

•

Why did it arrive when I was in the middle of an unrelated project? Just lucky, I guess.

> Particles of raw inspiration sleet through the
> universe all the time. Every once in a while

one of them hits a receptive mind, which then invents DNA or a flute sonata or a way to make light bulbs wear out in the half the time. But most of them miss.

— TERRY PRATCHETT, *Wyrd Sisters*

•

The formulation is a mashup of two metaphors. First, what if, in the treatment relationship, the patient functions as the right cerebral hemisphere of the brain and the clinician as the left? In brief, the right hemisphere creates, and the left analyzes. And second, what if the treatment is a creative work in progress cocreated by the patient and clinician in the same way the right and left hemispheres of a writer work together to create a novel? The creative process involves two phases: creation by the right hemisphere of a first draft containing a narrative arc, and revision of that draft by the left. These must be done separately or else stagnation, aka analysis paralysis, ensues.

Professional creators—people who make their living and way in the world by continually producing new narrative work (stories, symphonies, science experiments, choreographies)—use a deadline to consistently get a project started, as well as finished. Falling into the quicksand of procrastination before starting, and endless perfectionistic tweaking after without finishing are dangers that the deadline appears to mitigate.

The patient, functioning as right hemisphere in the treatment relationship, is responsible for delivering new material, as well as managing and closing the narrative arc of the session—its beginning, middle, and end—one option being the cliff-hanger, or doorknob moment.

The session's impending end is a deadline. Perhaps that structural element enables patients to reveal what they are afraid to reveal. That would mean the doorknob moment is not arbitrary. Rather, the deadline forcing a doorknob moment may be the only way the patient can deliver the revelation.

As a therapist, I live for the moment when the patient brings something new into the room. When patients (as right hemisphere) present me (as left) with new material, I analyze, reframe, and look for a way to help them integrate the revelation into the larger context of the ongoing treatment. Doing so, I broaden my own understanding of patients. Sharing that with them facilitates their understanding of themselves, which ideally moves the treatment forward.

In short, we *want* doorknob bombshells. That patients drop them reflects that they trust us to end the session on time. If we go with the assumption they wouldn't have told us otherwise, that confirms it is *therapeutic* to close as scheduled, even when the patient is distraught, even when it feels bad to do so.

•

This is not the first time an idea sleeting through the universe has hit me. But research in follow-up always revealed I'd arrived late to the party. Imagine my surprise at not finding anything definitive about the therapeutic value of ending on time in the literature on the doorknob moment. Chapter 1 covers that literature and serves as a counterpoint to and reference for the argument I advance in the rest of this book.

Chapter 2 gives a brief overview of the therapeutic core of the treatment relationship. Patients give us the power to influence their interpersonal environment and, by extension, their inner environment, which requires that they trust us. So much of what we do in therapy— providing a safe environment, establishing trust, exploring wishes, fantasies, and dreams—supports and encourages self-revelation. Self-disclosure is an absolute necessity in therapy. Without self-revelation, the patient will not benefit (Yalom, 2002). When a patient breaks new ground, especially when revealing something potentially shameful, embarrassing, incriminating, or traumatic—even when delivered inconveniently at the last minute—I now rejoice. Not only does this show that the patient trusts me, but the new material may also jump-start a new phase in the treatment.

Chapter 3 gets into the startling differences between the brain's two cerebral hemispheres in approach, attention, and agenda that each brings to our world. As a result, they are often in conflict, which drives how patients deliver information to us, including the doorknob moment.

Chapter 4 reviews professional artists' perspective on the creative process. Delivering new, original work leaves creatives vulnerable to public judgment in much the same way that patients' disclosures in treatment leave them exposed to us. The deadline helps them deliver despite that resistance, and it helps patients release what they need our help with.

Chapter 5 describes how conceptualizing the roles of patient and clinician in the treatment relationship as a metaphor for the functional differences between the right and left cerebral hemispheres yields a solid explanation for why doorknob moments occur, why they are necessary to prevent treatment stagnation, and why holding the deadline—ending on time—makes it safe for patients to deliver them. And since we can expect a range of doorknob bombshells in our practice, I also provide examples of the types I've experienced in mine and how I addressed them.

You'll see that it *is* therapeutic to end on time, which eliminates the need to make a last-minute judgment call. Your confidence in the therapeutic value of closing the session as scheduled will *check the natural impulse to run over* in the face of patient upset. Ending the session on time gracefully in the face of a patient's acute distress is a different but manageable challenge. You'll see what I mean through clinical examples.

•

You may wonder why I use "patient" instead of "client" when the two terms have become essentially interchangeable in the therapeutic literature. For me, "client" is far too transactional and generic a word to encompass the intimacy, vulnerability, and trust the therapy relationship requires. "Client" derives from the Latin *cliens*, to lean, in the sense of depend, while "patient" comes from the Latin *pati*, to suffer, and is perhaps akin to the Greek *pema*, suffering.

I vowed, when taking the Hippocratic Oath upon graduating medical school, to do no harm to those under my care. That is a moral commitment that demands I operate at the highest possible level of integrity and self-awareness, in order to rigorously avoid adding to patients' suffering. But that's just the foundation and the starting point. Our work, whenever possible, is to decrease patient suffering. So, "patient."

I also use the terms "psychoanalysis," "psychotherapy," and "therapy" interchangeably in this book, as well as "analyst" and "therapist."

CHAPTER 1

Is It Therapeutic to Always End on Time?

Opinion Is Mixed

Hardly any other profession functions in as
intimate and consistent an involvement with
time as does psychoanalysis. Considerations of
time figure prominently in our work.

— JACOB A. ARLOW, "Psychoanalysis and Time"

There I stand with my hand on the office doorknob,
Sarah sobbing her heart out next to me. Should I prolong the session, say, fifteen minutes, to take advantage
of this opportunity to process breakthrough material
she might suppress between sessions? Or, should I say
I'm sorry we don't have more time today and open the
door to usher her out? The first option will keep my
next patient waiting. But if I insist we end on time, will
that increase Sarah's suffering? I was taught as a res-

ident that it is therapeutic to end on time—but when the patient stands before me distraught, I always find myself asking . . . *is it*?

Doorknob bombshells seem to be inevitable, but there's no predicting them. When one hits, I always find making the judgment call—prolong the session? end as scheduled?—stressful. And I am not alone. "'Doorknob comments' are a phenomenon that may be relatively well developed in practice wisdom, but there is scant literature on the topic" (Arnd-Caddigan, 2013, p. 134).

Running late derails the day's schedule. At the least, it inconveniences or stresses the next scheduled patient, a complication that requires we process that with them. It's true that everything is grist for the therapy mill, but why add by beginning the session late? While highly motivating, these reasons don't actually answer the question of whether it helps or harms to end on time.

I turned to the literature for guidance. A review of the psychoanalysis, psychotherapy, psychiatry, social work, family practice, and primary care literature can be subdivided into three groups. All the psychotherapy articles focus on patient transference as a driver of doorknob moments, and their interpretation in that context, which then determined how to deal with them. The medical literature focuses on nonpsychodynamic drivers and research on how to make it easier for the patient to release sensitive information earlier in the session rather than at the end. The last group of five articles—Brody (2009), Arnd-Caddigan (2013), Wiggins (1983), Gans (2016), and Faden and Gorton (2018)—address "if and when it is appropriate to extend the session length in order to process these comments immediately or to defer this conversation until the next session. . . . [This] is an important clinical question" (Arnd-Caddigan, 2013, p. 134). Below I first address this last group of five articles, and then review articles analyzing last-minute comments from the psychoanalytic and psychotherapy literature, followed by articles on doorknob moments in medicine.

End on Time, or Extend the Session?

Stephanie Brody (2009) writes from intersubjective and existential perspectives about the effect of the end of the session on both analyst and patient. The final moments of the analytic hour are a repeating reenactment of disruption, separation, and loss. When this cocreated experience occurs without conscious awareness, avoidance and enactment (aka acting out) may occur. When it occurs in the context of shared understanding, the analytic pair may confront the "limitations and inevitabilities of life that are revived again and again when we approach and reach the end" (p. 90).

The interpersonal field of the analytic session activates many patterned experiences of attachments to important others, and disruptions of those attachments as well. These may constitute buried traumas for both patient and clinician, which "may reflect both the threats to the regulatory system resulting from separation as well as the response quality of the caregiver who observes or participates in the disruption" (Brody, 2009, p. 91). While this is readily obvious with longer interruptions, such as vacation, maternity leave, or illness,

> don't we [therapists] also feel the tug of anticipation as some sessions draw to a close? Some of us apologize. I know I do. "I'm sorry. I'm afraid we're out of time." Though we regard the separation as inevitable, the detachment [from the patient] can be painful. . . . *How often have we seen ourselves adjust the analytic boundary by giving more time, though we know the end has arrived?* [emphasis mine] How often do we struggle with the wish to reassure our

patients of our presence in their lives, even as we
are about to make our absence felt concretely? (p. 91)

This passage beautifully articulates why we are ambivalent about ending the session on time, especially if the
patient is acutely upset. Our empathy for the patient's
pain resonates with our own from past experiences,
and it is this human compassion, Brody implies, that
often drives the decision to give the patient more time.
Whether that benefits the treatment or not depends on
how the therapist processes the moment and returns it
to the treatment.

Margaret Arnd-Caddigan presents an intersubjective rationale for extending the session as a valid intervention for some patients. She suggests that the patient
and therapist cocreate the optimal therapeutic length
of the session, which is determined by what she calls
the patient's "internal [time] structure": the amount
of time the patient needs to both reveal and process
critical material. In this construct, doorknob moments
result when the patient's idiosyncratic internal time
structure is violated. The length of the session

is set after several sessions, and the amount of time
I schedule for each client may change as the internal

structure of the sessions changes. Recognizing and honoring the structure and rhythm of interactions with specific clients may reduce the incidence of "doorknob comments." (Arnd-Caddigan, 2013, p. 143)

Arnd-Caddigan addresses the various concerns this strategy raises. Will extending the session feed into the patient's unconscious fantasies of special treatment or status? Explicit discussion about the therapist's thoughts and motivations to extend the session with the patient is a necessary part of the jointly made decision. These exceptions to the standing time structure thus become part of the explored narrative of the treatment. Nothing is exempt from exploration in an analysis (Gutheil & Simon, 1995).

What about the clinician's schedule? What about the clients kept waiting? Arnd-Caddigan states that extending the session is the exception, not the rule, and in her experience the extension is usually brief—ten to fifteen minutes. Asking the patient if she has time to stay is simply respectful. And when the session is stretched into the next patient's appointment, that must be addressed and processed with the person who is kept waiting.

What about therapist countertransference? Why a therapist chooses to allow some clients to stay beyond

their regular session length always requires exploration. Is this an empathic response to the patient in
resonance with unavoidable existential realities, as
raised by Brody? Or is the therapist gratifying personal,
unconscious needs (Gutheil & Simon, 1995)? (More on
this below.)

Classical psychoanalyst Kenneth M. Wiggins (1983)
observes that people relate to time in a way that often
reflects their earlier relationships with authority figures
and their level of development. He supports occasionally extending the session length when the patient can
make positive use of a few extra minutes, so that "the
mental representation of that bit of time could be car-
ried with her as a reflection of the concern and regard
of her therapist" (p. 65).

Psychoanalyst Jerome S. Gans (2016), writing from
forty-seven years of experience, uses his countertransference reaction to a patient's doorknob disclosure to
help him decide whether to close or prolong the session.
His reaction helps him decode the transference subtext
underlying the patient's last-minute comment, which
then dictates the therapeutic next step.

Family practitioners Justin Faden and Gregg Gorton
(2018) focus pragmatically on the intensity of concern
aroused in the clinician, not the patient's level of dis-

tress, following a last-minute disclosure. If the remark is an isolated one, and the clinical urgency is high, "we would advocate for prolonging the encounter to ensure that the statement can be adequately addressed. Addressing concerns related to depression, self-injury, and suicide is paramount" (p. 53).

Transference, Countertransference, and the Doorknob Moment

The majority of the articles written about last-minute comments came from the psychoanalytic and psychotherapy literature. They focus primarily on psychodynamic reasons that patients drop critical information on their way out the door, the content of the last-minute disclosure, and its psychodynamic meaning specific to the patient, especially with regard to transference reactions around separation, loss, and endings. Countertransference reactions also play a significant role in the therapist's decision regarding how to manage the doorknob moment when it happens.

At a very young age we draw conclusions about and develop adaptations to important relationships and the world, which help us survive our childhood. Out of conscious awareness, we often continue using these conclusions and adaptations into adulthood, long past their shelf expiration date. (Psychoanalysts call this neurosis.) When these unexamined operating assumptions become crippling, people seek treatment. We attempt to help patients understand how relational disturbances they experience in the present are determined by events from the past (Arlow, 1986). More specifically, therapy helps patients grasp how adaptations from past relationships with important people manifest problematically in present life, and with the therapist as a transference.

Transference occurs when a patient transfers to the therapist feelings and fantasies attached to important people from early life. The essence of transference interpretation lies in its time dimension. "Patients love or hate their analysts. They envy, fear, or get angry with them not because of who their analysts really are, or what they do, but because they remind them of someone else in their early lives" (Hartocollis, 2003, pp. 950–951). Transference allows patients to express their feelings from a significant relationship in early life with the therapist in the here and now of the analytic situation. When the analyst provides an interpretation—makes a connection between the patient's past experience with the actual experience in real time in the therapy relationship—this gives the patient the opportunity to expand his understanding of the past relationship in the context of the present therapy relationship *as it never could have been experienced were it not for the analysis* [emphasis mine]" (p. 952).

In other words, the patient's transference relationship with the therapist exists in the present but is also colored by an older relationship from the past, the memory of which remains in the timelessness of the unconscious, unless the analyst directs the patient's attention to it with an interpretation that links the patient's present behavior with the analyst to that of someone in the past. Only by consistently exploring their interplay can past and present come together in the patient's mind in a new way.

Thus the process of therapy reconstructs memory by revising, expanding, and updating the meaning given to the original experience.

The most widely referenced paper of this group, published by psychoanalyst Glen O. Gabbard (1982), suggests that "exit lines"—patients' last words before leaving—"may be the most important communication of the hour, conveying a message that the patient feels he cannot say on the couch or in the chair" (p. 580). The material embedded in exit lines deserves careful attention because, Gabbard notes, the patient is unlikely to bring it up in the next session. The patient says the exit line while leaving because he wants to keep it out of the session.

> More exactly, the patient is ambivalent about communicating this material. . . . Hurling it as a parting shot is a compromise between saying it and not saying it. The communication is often so emotionally charged that it can only be conveyed to the analyst as the session ends, *where a breather from the situation will follow* [emphasis mine]. (p. 580)

Whenever I discuss doorknob moments with colleagues, this is the explanation that always comes up, heads nodding in agreement, because it makes intuitive sense.

An exit line may carry many meanings, some specific to the patient's transference to the therapist, such as allowing her to continue having a fantasized relationship with the therapist outside/after the session. Or vice versa: the intent of the exit line may be to make the therapist think about the patient after the session is over. Or the exit line is a fantasized triumph over the finite limits of the session, or a defense against it.

The [impending] separation is passively experienced, and the act of standing at the end of the session provides a certain feeling of being in control and active. It is from this active position that the patient hurls a parting shot to defend against the passivity and helplessness of being abandoned. (Gabbard, 1982, pp. 586–587)

Gabbard grouped exit lines into patterns that he named the curtain call, the last-second question, the stereotyped exit, the attempt to censor unacceptable material, the cry for help, and making reparations.

My patient Sarah's last-minute bombshell was a cry for help. Because she had to pass through the waiting room to exit (where the next patient waited), I didn't have the heart to let her leave while actively crying. So, I offered her tissues, reassured her we would talk about this at the next session if she wanted, and gave her a few minutes to pull herself together.

While this was happening, my next scheduled patient, Jack (Type A, hyperpunctual, hair-trigger temper) became irate at being kept waiting. He spent the first fifteen minutes of his session berating me for wasting his time, my sloppy time management, lack of professionalism, and so on. However, in the last five minutes of the session, he backtracked and apologized for his earlier, harshly judgmental words, saying he'd gone too far. Clearly, he was anxious he had strained our therapeutic alliance and was making reparations.

The end of each hour is a separation. This structural element often triggers the patient to reexperience endings and losses from earlier in life just as the session's end forecasts the impending loss of the therapist. Thus, exit lines tend to make latent transference issues overt. My keeping Jack waiting for his session triggered the rage and helplessness he had felt as a boy when his mother arrived hours late to pick him up from school, events, or a friend's house or, worse, didn't show at all. He remembers shouting at her furiously, which she'd ignore, then turn her back, and leave the room. He'd become frightened and anxious by her withdrawal, and repeatedly apologize. This cycle of anger and exit line reparations played out in the treatment, where, unlike with his mother, we processed it until he slowly gained perspective.

In short, the number of ways patients use exit lines is as various as their psychopathologies and their defensive strategies. The patient may throw an exit line as a way to make the therapist feel guilty, or to express anger, or it might be the only way an inhibited patient can reveal uncomfortable information. In its many forms, the last-minute comment can be clearly understood as a defense against the many feelings evoked by the experience of separation.

> Final words are heavily invested because they bear the feelings deriving from earlier separations. . . . [They] are saved for the hour's end to keep them out of the therapeutic process and to render the therapist impotent and unable to respond. However, the therapist need not despair because he can bring these comments into the following hour as the focus of more productive work. (Gabbard, 1982, p. 597)

Psychoanalyst Peter Hartocollis (2003) speaks to the analyst's maintenance of the structural regularity and predictability of each session. The session's duration becomes a routine that the patient takes for granted, "so much so that he or she soon surrenders its control to the analyst." Therefore, he concludes,

> it is a matter of resistance, to be interpreted in terms of the patient's transference neurosis, when the boundaries of time agreed upon are disregarded or

manipulated by the patient: when the patient misses sessions; or arrives late . . . or brings up dreams or other important material near the end of the session in an obvious effort either to prolong its duration or not deal with such material. (p. 941)

Is the patient's release of critical information at the last minute *simply* a matter of resistance? Are the patient's motivations truly obvious? The language of this paragraph is subtly judgmental, as if the patient's resistance is getting in the way of the work. But dealing with resistance *is* the work. Perhaps resistance is facilitated or unmasked by the analyst reliably ending on time.

J. S. Gans (2016), a relational therapist, notes that, like many other apparently simple phenomena, "the ending of a psychotherapy session is relationally actually very complex" (p. 413). "Just as the patient's exit line may have extraordinary significance to the therapist, the therapist's parting comment may have similar significance to the patient" (Gabbard, 1982, p. 596). Gans (2016) agrees with Gabbard that exit lines are indicators of the patient's psychopathology but observes that Gabbard "pays scant attention to the analyst's contribution to their patients' parting shots" (p. 415).

The spontaneous, unpredictable, and distinctive nature of last-minute patient–therapist exchanges defies consistency. This is why attending to session-ending relational matters is important. Many factors, for both patient and therapist, may play a role in the final moments of a session. These include character, history (especially with separation, loss, and attachment), developmental level, context, phase of therapy, state of the therapeutic alliance, transference and countertransference, and the degree of therapist emotional attunement and/or empathic failure that has characterized the session.

The final moments of the hour are a repetitive reenactment whose symbolic meaning can be both a challenge and an opportunity for therapist and patient. Both are vulnerable to the revival of feelings and memories of deprivation and loss aroused by the impending end of the session (Arnd-Caddigan, 2013; Brody, 2009; Gans, 2016; Wiggins, 1983).

These clinical challenges call on the therapist to be variously creative, authentic, empathic, firm, nonjudgmental, and introspective, all in the service of avoiding shaming the patient and providing for optimal responsiveness. Achieving these goals is a real challenge. Psychotherapists in private practice get left approximately eight times a day and can become inured to the emotional reverberations that these mini-separations create. (Gans, 2016, p. 426)

(In my combined medication-management/psychotherapy practice I get left more often than that! As do non-mental health clinicians.) A therapist finding herself wanting to either prolong the session or end it early, or actually doing so, must search for and examine unconscious attitudes—countertransference reactions—she may have towards the patient (Wiggins, 1983).

The classical psychoanalytic position regarding ending on time, while not explicitly stated, is that the analyst ends the session as scheduled, regardless of last-minute revelations. The exit line then serves the dual purpose of closing the current session while functioning as a bridge to the next, when its contextual, transferential, or psychodynamic meaning will be processed (Gabbard, 1982; Gans, 2016). Thus, in the wake of the exit line, the psychoanalyst's immediate task is to sensitively send the patient on his way, without addressing it. Therapists especially attuned to patients with trauma history may take special pains to make sure these patients don't get retraumatized by the session's ending.

Suppose such a patient, with five minutes left in the session, embarks on a particularly sensitive or shame-filled topic. Asking, "Would it be better to wait until the next session to talk about this material?" may help the patient avoid further emotional injury. (Gans, 2016, p. 419)

Psychoanalyst Robert M. Waugaman (1992) uses the term "analytic time" to describe the unique qualities of the patient's experience of time in the context of treatment. The time frame of an analysis—its initiation, duration, and termination—may stir the patient to experience various unconscious associations and repetitions. So will other aspects of analytic time, such as the beginning and end of the session, and the analyst's schedule (Waugaman, 1992).

The therapy itself may be experienced by the patient as a recapitulation of earlier historical developmental phases: the beginning of the treatment, birth and the early years; the middle, entry of sibs and loss of parents; and its end, a symbolic death. Anniversary reactions are an example of how we unconsciously track specific times, their clinical significance, and their emotional meaning. The therapy presents the apparent paradox of "a 'timeless' unconscious that can nonetheless tell time" (Waugaman, 1992, p. 40). (More on this and the right cerebral hemisphere in Chapter 3.)

The "frame," or framework of the session, provides a fixed, predictable structure in which the analysis unfolds. Robert Langs (1984) argued that the frame has been greatly neglected in the literature, although he considers it to be "the single most fundamental component of the analytic and therapeutic interactions. . . " (Waugaman, 1992, p. 44). The analytic frame separates treatment from the rest of reality, giving it its unique and illusory qualities. Time constitutes a major dimension of the frame, since it defines the frequency and length of sessions, as well as the total length of the treatment. Not only does the patient react to analytic time as part of the frame, but he also sees it as what he pays the analyst for: the analyst's time (Waugaman, 1992).

The importance of the frame stems partly from its role in establishing the safety and security of the analytic situation. Langs (1977) argues that the patient's transference reaction is most often directed *toward the frame*: to whether it is secure—beginning and ending on time—or deviant. The framework can be thought of as process, and may sometimes take precedence over the actual content of the session. Its

importance can be easily overlooked when the therapist becomes preoccupied with content and ignores
the more silent aspects of the process. Countertransference needs may also lead the analyst to neglect the
frame, that is, to shorten or prolong the session. Maintaining the integrity of the session time frame is one
precondition for creating a safe therapeutic environment (Waugaman, 1992).

Because the analytic setting functions as a means of
facilitating entry into another person's reality, setting a
variety of boundaries provides the conditions of safety
that will enable the patient to experience the analyst
as a representative of multiple levels of reality. Brody
(2009) describes these as follows.

Free association allows the patient to cross the
boundary between conscious inhibition and unconscious expression. Interpretation allows us to cross the
boundary between our own experience of the patient
and the patient's experience of himself. Transference
allows us to cross the boundary between the patient's
past and present. The transference relationship is what
Freud called "a path to the awakening of memories."
It is the medium through which psychic time may be
processed (Brody, 2009).

With its structured beginning, middle, and end, the

analytic hour activates many patterned experiences related to attachment and separation—what Brody calls "hidden traumas of infancy"—for both patient and therapist. Even though the separation followed by the session's end is inevitable, detaching can be painful. Without reflection, we are vulnerable to acting out by extending the session.

> How often have we seen ourselves adjust the analytic boundary by giving more time, though we know the end has arrived? ... We hope we are present in our patient's inner world, even as we underscore our absence in their day-to-day real-life experience. If our patients struggle with aloneness, they will struggle with the end of the session. (Brody, 2009, p. 91)

The absence of secure attachment to important others in the past can make traversing the space between the session and its end particularly difficult for the patient.

> Each encounter asserts the possibility of connection in the context of psychic aloneness. We cannot avoid these feelings. In fact, we replay them over and

over. But now, we are in it, together. . . . We are in
a moment that evokes the old but how we handle it
allows for a new, contrasting experience to combine
with that memory and change it. (Brody, 2009, p. 93)

(Memories are not stored by the brain in a fixed form
but instead are reconstructed at will—perhaps this is
why the therapist's interpretation of transference reactions can prove game-changing for the patient. More on
memory in Chapter 3.)

The ending of every session mirrors death and
loss—"The End"—as does the end of a treatment. My
middle-aged patient Clara, who had survived a horrific
childhood of neglect and physical and sexual abuse, suffered intense grief and crushing feelings of abandon-
ment when her long-time therapist retired. She didn't
think she would survive the loss; she was sure she'd
never find another therapist; she was sure I would
reject her, too.

Instead, I provided continuity and stability, which
enabled her to process the loss. She had been seeing me
once a month for medication management of her severe
posttraumatic stress disorder (PTSD), but I increased
the frequency of contact to once a week. I lengthened
her session from twenty minutes to forty-five to pro-

vide a combined supportive/insight-oriented therapy until she settled, which took a couple years. Despite several appeals, her health insurance eventually declined to pay me as a psychiatrist to provide psychotherapy. Because I continued to manage her medications (with a side of supportive therapy), she tolerated the change and was able to find a new therapist, with whom she bonded strongly.

When "The End" occurs in the absence of awareness by both patient and therapist, acting out and avoidance can result.

> But when it occurs within a context of shared understanding, the analytic pair is free to intensify, play with, and confront the limitations and inevitabilities of life that are revived again and again as we approach and reach the end [of the session]. This is the point in the process, as children and adults, where "it takes courage to face reality." (Brody, 2009, p. 94)

It takes courage to face our awareness of loss and the impermanence of life, and to pair it with the desire to go on—perhaps, Brody suggests, even to thrive. How do we therapists bear the pain of reliving our own losses while also bearing the pain of our patients? What makes it possible for us to journey beyond our own into others' painful places (Brody, 2009)?

The great Erich Fromm (1998) defined what it takes to be a good therapist as follows. The therapist must be empathic and strong enough to feel the other's experience as if it were their own. Further, this empathy is a crucial facet of the capacity for love. To understand another is to love him—not in the erotic sense, but in the sense of reaching out to him and overcoming the fear of losing oneself. Finally, understanding and love are inseparable. If they are separate, it is a cerebral process and the door to essential understanding remains closed.

Perhaps it is the therapy relationship itself, with its bond of deep attachment and love, that enables patient and therapist to travel together. Perhaps, also, being together is what makes the journey possible. Perhaps, more deeply, this is simply a truth of any love-based human connection. This insight came to me after I became separated from my husband and son while visiting the Holocaust Museum in Washington, DC, and went through most of the exhibits alone. By the end, I was sickened and overwhelmed by a dark despair. *If I ever find myself terrified and trapped like that, I'll kill myself,* I decided, *as my last act of defiance and self-control.* Surfacing from those depths, I heard music coming from somewhere out of sight. Steven Spielberg's documentary of survivor interviews was playing in an open auditorium. I took a seat, lost myself in it, and could hardly tear myself away when my husband and son found me—"We've been looking all over for you!" My spirit was remarkably uplifted. Why? Despite the horror, each survivor had cared about someone else there, and that was enough to keep them going. My decision to end it all assumed I would be ripped away from my family, friends, and community; that I would be isolated, disconnected, and untethered; that I would be alone at the mercy of the apocalypse. But what if I was wrong about that? What if I made a friend who had my back, and I theirs? Maybe, then, I would choose to endure.

The human connection is an awe-inspiring mystery. Even in the hell of a concentration camp, people bond to support one another. Brody suggests that it is the therapist's experience, awareness, and sensitivity to these core existential paradoxes—the impending loss embedded in connection, death in life—that make us vulnerable to acting out by extending the session. But these also create an openness to the psychic suffering—our own and our patients'—of grief, aloneness, and finality. "How do we bear this? What makes it possible for us to journey to these terribly painful places? . . . Together it is possible" (Brody, 2009, p. 95).

The intensity of the work often induces a change in the sense of the time. That it is moving either slowly or swiftly during a session "has its explanation in the vicissitudes of transference" (Hartocollis, 2003, p. 953). Therapists are not exempt: our sense of time may be affected as well and be reflected in a countertransference-fueled disregard for the boundaries of time. Both unexamined dislike and positive regard for the patient can manifest as the analyst extending the session for more than a few minutes in order to avoid the guilt aroused by the first, and pleasure by the second, among other affects (Hartocollis, 2003).

There is no downside to paying attention to the therapeutic possibilities embedded in session endings. In the cocreated moment of ending, adjusting the length of the session without self-awareness of our own needs and hidden traumas can begin the slippery slide into more egregious boundary violations. In 1913, Sigmund Freud observed that some patients viewed comments made when not lying on the couch—in other words, when arriving and leaving—as separate from the formal treatment. He advised the analyst not to accept this artificial separation but to "take note of what is said before or after the session and . . . [to] bring it forward at the first opportunity, thus pulling down the partition which the patient has tried to erect" (Gutheil & Simon, 1995, p. 337).

Thomas G. Gutheil and Robert I. Simon (1995) similarly note that interactions in the transition zones between chair and door appear to somehow be held separate from the therapy hour by both patient and clinician, and that the consequences can be dire. Damaging boundary violations begin insidiously in this space and may progress if unexplored; patients and therapists are more vulnerable to committing boundary excursions and violations in this zone (Guthiel & Simon, 1995).

Content particularly vulnerable to immunity from exploration in session includes bill paying, appointment scheduling, and prescription writing. "Such areas are always in danger of being scanted by both therapists and patients prone to avoiding the many conflictual issues latent in these interactions" (Gutheil & Simon, 1995, p. 337). Therefore, it is important to note countertransference feelings around administrative and logistical details (patient arriving late, receiving/not receiving payment, etc.). Insights about the patient's psychopathology resulting from an examination of countertransference reactions should be brought into the treatment for exploration, especially if the patient's behaviors occur in the transition zone before or after the technical end of the session.

Delegating fee collection and scheduling to a receptionist or office manager frees up session time for clinical work. But doing so also spreads the patient's transference away from us onto staff, who may or may not let us know. I had a patient who canceled several of her standing appointments by voice mail to schedule other medical appointments during our time. Because I have my office manager document voice mail cancellations in the chart, I noted the pattern when the patient next came in and brought it up in session. In our physician-shortage area, it *is* objectively difficult to schedule medical appointments, so I wasn't surprised when she said, "If I didn't take the appointment, I would have had to wait for months!" Yet the pattern was new, so I asked her, "Why now? We're going through a rough patch in the treatment. Are you finding you don't want to come in?" Which, no surprise, was the case.

Either patient or therapist may functionally extend the appointment without directly addressing the wish either has for more time. The space is treated as a free zone, as if it doesn't count as part of the therapy in determining the length of the hour or the material explored. Sessions may gradually lengthen in time, and from there, the therapist may intentionally reschedule appointments to the end of the day, "a move that sometimes represents a way station on the path to sexual misconduct" (Gutheil & Simon, 1995, p. 337).

The transition zone before the session is just as vulnerable to boundary violations as the zone after. Having just revealed sensitive information about her marriage, my patient Jane had bolted, weeping, from my office through the waiting room to the exit. My next patient, Harry, watched her rush out, stood up, followed me into the office, and remained standing while I shut the door. "People keep leaving your office crying! It's a trend!" he said. "What did you do to that poor woman?"

"Not telling," I said, smiling, lifting my hand to point at his chair, and moving to mine.

"Maybe I should get another shrink!" He joked uneasily as he sat down. Was he annoyed I'd thwarted his invitation to blur the treatment boundary and betray Jane's confidence? Maybe. More likely, he was anxious that I might have the power to make him cry, too. I chose to fish and responded concretely, "Really? You're thinking of leaving? Are you upset with me?" As it happens, he was.

Then there is the transition from the chair to door. My patient Jake, who had a solo landscaping business said, as I walked him out of my office, "I have to tell you, whoever is working on your property doesn't know what he's doing." My heart immediately sank. Three businesses had already bailed on the project. I sighed and walked outside with him, where he explained what was wrong and what he would do differently. A wave of desperation to get the job done plus my positive countertransference—I fell for Jake's pitch—led me to hire him to take on the job. You'd think being in practice for twenty-plus years, I'd have known better. Yeah, you'd think that.

Of course, the situation was untenable and quickly deteriorated. He juggled my project with another simultaneously, making me grind my teeth in exasperation. *Get my job done!* Overuse and inattention to injuries of his back and elbows plagued him, worsening his psychiatric symptoms. Horror overtook me—he was mismanaging and hurting himself doing this job for me. Admittedly, he would have done that with any client and (*duh*) that was one reason he was in treatment. As a healer, my primary commitment is to do no harm, no exceptions, so I took him off the job. With my needs back where they belonged, dealing with just his felt like a vacation.

Elements of the analytic situation, such as the open-endedness of its overall duration and the frequency and fixed time of its session, conditioned as they are by the concept of time, contribute to the development of transference and its various manifestations, including those of countertransference. (Hartocollis, 2003, p. 944)

Because doing psychotherapy brings up covert, unconscious, or unintended wishes in the therapist, the potential for acting out is ever present throughout the treatment and can lead to mismanagement of those pesky doorknob moments.

Doorknob Moments in Medicine

Several articles focus on preventing doorknob moments and what clinicians can do to make it easier for patients to reveal difficult information earlier in the session, instead of at the end, thus (theoretically) eliminating the doorknob moment as a management issue. With the exception of the article by psychotherapist Arnd-Caddigan (2013), discussed above, these came from the primary care literature.

Primary care physicians are under tremendous pressure to address the multiple, complex medical comorbidities of an aging population within the time-limited appointment frame forced on them by health insurance carriers. Surprise—primary care patients, like mental health patients, also reveal critical information at the last minute of the appointment, regardless of the length of the appointment. In fact, the term "doorknob syndrome" was coined by urologist Graham Jackson (2005) to refer to patients who report alarming symptoms as they leave the appointment, usually opening with, "Oh, by the way. . . ." He observes that patients are not always forthcoming about what really motivates them to visit their doctor. "How do we tease out these 'by the way' moments which may be important clinically and whatever their clinical significance *are always important to the patient*? [emphasis mine]" (Jackson, 2005, p. 869).

Jackson is a kind man; all his strategies are solidly grounded in the social and interpersonal skills that put people at ease. His simplest strategy to make it easier for patients to reveal their concerns earlier in the session is to just ask directly if they have any: "How can I help? Do you have anything on your mind we haven't covered yet?" (Jackson, 2005, p. 869). He notes that humor

is an important component of medicine and certainly relaxes the consultation. . . . Laughter can be
key to opening-up an often difficult subject, as does
listening carefully with good eye contact [emphasis
mine]. . . . Listening to a patient whilst focusing on
a computer screen is a deterrent to the patient opening-up to what the problem really is. (p. 869)

It is important, Jackson notes, to make time for the
patient and to resist administrative pressure to see more
people by spending less time with each.

Patients are often frightened, worried, and need
time—our decision-making process still depends on
a good history. . . . I do not know if this approach
reduces the "doorknob" problem, but it does allow
an opening for that suppressed but critical com-
plaint or worry. (p. 869)

One study found that about two-thirds of the time medically complex patients and their physicians agreed on
the priorities to be accomplished during an appointment (Kowalski, 2018). When they differed, patients
typically prioritized discussing current symptoms while

physicians prioritized guideline-based prevention and chronic disease management. When the communication between the two was suboptimal, patients had worse adherence and poorer clinical outcomes.

Previsit preparation by both was an important contributor to alignment. Patients noted two barriers to alignment of priorities: short visit lengths and difficulty in raising sensitive concerns. Sensitive concerns included sexual dysfunction, blood in stool, anxiety, panic attacks, depression, suicidal ideation, substance abuse, and housing issues (Kowalski, 2018).

Physicians agreed with patients on the challenges of limited visit time and the need to establish priorities from a longer list of concerns. Many physicians described feeling stressed by the issues and reported they often went over allotted appointment time to address as many of the patient's concerns as possible. Patients reported feeling valued that their physician would take the extra time when necessary while also expressing awareness that the next patient would be kept waiting (Kowalski, 2018).

This study concluded that patient delays in raising concerns or physician inability to elicit them early in the visit led to new information coming to light at the end of the visit. Time constraints and medical complexity "require patients and physicians to implement proactive strategies early in the visit to better manage their limited time together" (Kowalski, 2018, p. 8). Given the average patient's lack of solid medical information and the cognitive impairment that accompanies stress and anxiety, I believe this asks too much of most patients. And given how tightly scheduled physicians are by practice managers, preparing ahead of time for a patient, especially a complex one, is all too often not possible.

Another study concluded that technology-based interventions hold "great promise for improving the patient experience in primary care" (Wittink et al., 2018, p. 13), though successful adoption requires interventions to be unobtrusive and brief. A software tool such as Customized Care could be made available through patient portals, or on smartphones, to prime the patient–physician discussion, especially for stigmatized topics such as mental or sexual health, potentially making the office visit more efficient (Wittink et al., 2018).

I find this conclusion unrealistically optimistic. Questionnaires mediated by technology cannot replace the trust built in real time between a patient and a competent clinician who listens with a sympathetic ear. Additionally, this model has the implicit bias of privilege built into it. Internet access is hardly uniform across the country. In my rural town, many of my patients don't have access to reliable internet service, and many can't afford a smartphone. Additionally, the most medically complex patients tend to be elderly, and this demographic is least likely to be internet savvy.

"Research has focused on how to elicit these statements earlier in the visit to curb the doorknob moment phenomenon. However, few resources discuss strategies for how to address doorknob moments after they are made" (Faden & Gorton, 2018, p. 53). Faden and Gorton open their paper with an all-too-common scenario: The patient exits the appointment saying, in an exasperated tone, " 'If this doesn't work, I may just kill myself!' Is it appropriate to prolong the session to discuss this comment? Why do patients always seem to say things or ask questions when they are leaving the exam room?" (p. 52). Physicians' reactions to the sense of powerlessness induced by these unwelcome last-minute comments span the range of dysphoric affects, from frustration to annoyance, resentment, or even anger (Faden & Gorton, 2018). (This is also true for mental health clinicians, but we are trained to consider our emotional reactions to patients—aka countertransference—as data that may be useful to the treatment.)

Nonpsychoanalytic reasons for a patient extending the appointment include primary gain (gratification derived from the sick role), loneliness (the appointment is the social highlight of the patient's day, week, month . . .), and/or anger (wanting to punish the doctor for the appointment being too short). Faden and Gorton (2018) acknowledge that these strategies all ensure the physician continues thinking about the patient after the appointment has ended, which prolongs the appointment in the patient's mind, if not in real time.

They also note that patients may use the transition of exiting the room as an opportunity to blur the professional boundary with last-minute personal questions that catch the clinician off guard. Such questions are an attempt to shift the paradigm and the power dynamic of the physician-patient relationship and reshape it into another kind of relationship—friendship, business adviser, or romantic partner, to name a few (Faden & Gorton, 2018). As discussed earlier, Gutheil and Simon (1995) advise that such incursions in the transition zone should not be ignored but explored in the treatment. If they remain unacknowledged by both patient and clinician, the risk for serious ethical boundary violations, such as sexual misconduct, goes up.

Psychoanalyst Gans (2016) suggests clinicians should

delay answering a patient's unexpected, last-minute question, especially if it is of a personal nature and makes the clinician uneasy.

> [The patient asks], "Will you miss me?" Taken by surprise, her therapist had the presence of mind to say, "You have a way of saving important questions for the end of the session. Let's begin next session with your question." Her therapist was relieved . . . because his present feeling was "not much." (p. 425)

The therapist, upon examining his countertransference response at leisure, then had a critical insight into the patient's psychopathology and went on to figure out the most tactful way to deliver that insight at a later time in the treatment (Gans, 2016).

When a patient makes a suicidal comment at the end of a session, discerning whether it reflects actual intent to self-harm requires significant clinical experience in general, and with the patient in particular. Gans (2016) provides an example of a patient who said he felt suicidal in the last moments of the session before Gans took a vacation. Gans, trusting his gut, assessed his countertransference response as a reflection of the patient's cry for help: "Fred want[ed] to make sure I didn't forget about him when I went on vacation" (p. 425). He did not prolong the session beyond giving Fred this interpretation with the reassurance they would talk about it when he got back. The patient subsequently confirmed that Gans had deciphered his suicidal comment correctly.

Faden and Gorton (2018) suggest that the intensity of concern aroused in the clinician should guide the clinician's decision whether to lengthen the session time or not. If the clinical urgency is high, they feel extending the session to adequately address concerns related to suicidality and self-harm is a must. "Spending the additional time can bolster rapport and benefit patient care" (p. 53). Prolonging an appointment to parse out whether the patient was merely frustrated or truly at wit's end when saying she might kill herself conveys "in an empathic manner that you are both in this together. Taking the time to do so can be the difference between hope and trust, and despair and isolation" (p. 53).

Unlike psychiatric and therapy patients who expect to be seen on time, family practice and primary care patients are used to their doctors running late and keeping them waiting. Given that, this is a reasonable intervention that probably won't strain (within reason) the therapeutic alliance with the waiting patient. To be respectful of the waiting patient's time, if the delay will be prolonged, it's a good idea to offer to reschedule.

If the doorknob remark is part of a pattern, and clinical concern is low, Faden and Gorton (2018) feel it may be appropriate to defer addressing it until the next appointment. Regardless, they advise erring on the side of caution.

Summary

The issue with doorknob moments is that they are unexpected, often alarming, and happen when the appointment is technically over as the patient is leaving. Clinicians must quickly assess the relevant variables to determine what the patient's communication means, and then decide how to handle it, usually with the next patient kept waiting.

Did this review answer the question *Is it therapeutic to end on time, even if the patient is distraught in the wake of a doorknob revelation?* Well, yes and no. The only unambiguous scenario is when the patient uses language that suggests self-harm or suicide—then the answer to the question is a definite no. The message is clear, whether explicit, as in the medical literature, or implicit, as in the psychotherapy literature, that we must always take time with patients to figure out if they mean to hurt themselves or not.

Five articles discussed the therapeutic value of lengthening the session after a last-minute disclosure, a decision made on a case-by-case basis. Overall, the psychoanalytic literature assumes the therapist ends the session on time, deferring discussion of the door-knob moment to the next session. The logistics of doing that therapeutically requires understanding the comment in the context of the patient's transference and therapist countertransference.

Treating the "free zone" between door and chair as separate from the appointment can lead to its lengthening without acknowledgment by patient or clinician. If countertransference remains unexamined, this can escalate to more egregious boundary violations harmful to the patient. All exchanges both on the way in and on the way out of the appointment must be brought back into the treatment, ideally within the designated appointment time.

What about the question of *why* doorknob moments happen? Psychoanalyst Gabbard noted that "exit lines" aren't random but are a function of the patient's psychopathology and transference to the therapist. Moreover, they can be categorized into types, which can be identified in different patients (the cry for help, the curtain call, among others). In the medical population, non-transference motivators for parting comments (loneliness, discomfort bringing up sensitive concerns, among others) also separate into identifiable patterns across large numbers of patients.

Finally, can doorknob moments be eliminated? We'd like the answer to be yes, but it seems unlikely, given that may be the only way some patients can release sensitive information. Only Arnd-Caddigan (2013), from the psychoanalytic literature, suggests a construct that *may* decrease the incidence of doorknob moments, which involves lengthening the session with highly nuanced consideration of transference and countertransference issues, as well as being willing to process the fallout with the patient that is kept waiting as a result.

Two studies used internet technology and smartphones for previsit preparation to facilitate clinicians and patients working together to address patients' concerns during, rather than at the end of, the appointment. Results were mixed, with clinicians tending to run over time to address complex concerns.

I hope this review has been helpful in confirming what you already know and what you are already doing.

But did it quell the doubt that ending on time might cause the patient more suffering? Did it confirm that ending on time really *is* therapeutic when a patient is sobbing heartbrokenly before us after revealing something deeply painful at the last minute? There is a felt sense that the answer to both questions is yes, but certainty remains just outside the spotlight of clarity, hovering in shadow.

CHAPTER 2

The Cocreated Therapy Relationship

Agent of Change

In contrast to Freud's drive theory, which suggests a developing individual is largely controlled by the expression of built-in drives, or instincts, the neo-Freudians Harry Stack Sullivan, Donald W. Winnicott, Karen Horney, and Irvin D. Yalom credited the shaping of character throughout life to the influence of the interpersonal environment an individual is embedded within. As Winnicott, pediatrician and psychoanalyst, noted in 1947: *There is no such thing as a baby, there is a baby and someone.* More recently, Allan N. Schore (2019), from the field of interpersonal neurobiology, has said essentially the same: "The organizing principle of this developmental relational conception dictates that 'the self-organization of the developing brain occurs in the context of a relationship with another brain'" (p. 17).

In *The Art of Listening*, Erich Fromm (1998) conceptualized understanding and love as inseparable to the therapist's engagement with patients. If they are separate, it is a cerebral process and the door to essential understanding remains closed. Schore (2019) describes Freud's fallout with his early disciple Sándor Ferenczi as arising over the issue of love. Freud tended to eroticize all forms of adult love, while Ferenczi, through a process he called "mutual analysis," established the centrality of mutual emotional experience generally, and love specifically, between patient and therapist.

> For Ferenczi, the essential characteristics of parenthood were the essential characteristics of the psychotherapist.... Love, one of the most powerful emotions, fits better into contemporary, relational psychoanalysis, a two-person psychology wherein intersubjectivity is both the goal and the medium for transformation.... Our clinical theories call for and make use of the analyst's emotional responsiveness—in particular, the analyst's capacity to love authentically and use his love therapeutically. (p. 179)

A patient gives the therapist the power to influence her interpersonal environment and, by extension, her inner environment, which requires she trust the therapist. This chapter reviews elements essential to the building, care, and maintenance of trust in a viable therapeutic relationship, the bedrock of our work.

Facilitating Aha Moments

I have been particularly influenced by Karen Horney's *Neurosis and Human Growth: The Struggle Toward Self-Realization*, in which she argues that humans have a built-in propensity toward self-realization. Therapy helps remove the obstacles—intrapsychic and interpersonal—that hold back or impede self-awareness, liberating a person to develop into their mature, self-actualized self, just as an acorn grows into an oak tree when the necessary nutrients are available.

If a psychotherapy treatment is successful, the patient, upon ending treatment, is competent to continue the process on her own in an ongoing self-analysis. This is the rationale behind the need for beginning therapists to engage in a training analysis. Therapists' personal limitations or lack of self-awareness limits their clinical effectiveness, just as a chain is only as strong as its weakest link. Moreover, in aging through the life cycle, the ever-evolving therapist may return for another course of treatment to speed the process of removing new or recurring obstacles. (Lay people may, too, of course.)

Many of Horney's formulations of core intrapsychic drivers that lead to neurosis—distortions of self-identity that lead to dysfunctional interpersonal relations—have proven themselves evergreen. When a person turns a wish or a need (that may in fact be reasonable) into a claim of entitlement, this creates relationship trouble and personal suffering. For example, we may wish or need a plane to depart on time because we have a conference to attend. It's okay to want this, but we are not entitled to it. The difference between a need and a claim is clear-cut, but patients are often not only unaware of the difference but also averse to seeing it.

By turning a need unwittingly into a claim, the person assumes the irrational stance of assuming a right that in reality does not exist. This entitlement leads to the formation of an idealized, false self. This false self's primary work is to repel the intrusion of reality, which confronts its validity. How this manifests is unique to each individual, but denial of reality leads inevitably to interpersonal difficulties, which is what brings the person to seek therapy (Horney, 1950).

My patient Jim, sixty-two, had been in treatment for almost twenty years when the COVID-19 pandemic swept the country (and our town) in March of 2020. Hundreds of thousands of people were dying. Life-saving vaccines had not yet come out. Businesses shut down, and the Centers for Disease Control and Prevention (CDC) mandated a nationwide "sheltering in place." Seeing patients in person simply was not an option.

Yet Jim became increasingly angry—he hated having his session by phone or video chat. He repeatedly demanded I see him in the office. I agreed with him that remote contact was a poor second best to being together. Still, I said, it was far better than no treatment at all. Jim dismissed that. His understandable need and wish had become an entitlement. He expected me to ignore the CDC's public health mandate and waive my office policy. He actually said—I am not making this up—"I never go out. Trust me, I won't bring the virus into the office." *I'm special*, his idealized self insisted. *Reality does not apply to me and, by extension, you.*

Jim's rigid adherence to righteous and unreasonable expectations of the important people in his life was a long-standing source of suffering and a theme of our work together. Jim's false self needed me to validate his claim of entitlement in order to actualize itself in relation to the outside world. When I pointed out that he was asking me to put my life at risk—something I wouldn't do for him or for anyone—he left treatment.

Psychotherapy work is inherently complex, because any person's internal adaptations, self-illusions, and entitlements function to protect them from perceived dangers, whether internal or external, and we cling to these as tenaciously as a shipwreck survivor adrift at sea clings to a life preserver. There is only so much we can do, Horney (1950) says.

> We must be clear about the seriousness of the involvement [of intrapsychic defenses] in order to guard against false optimism, envisioning quick and easy cures. In fact the word "cure" is appropriate only as long as we think of a relief of symptoms, like a phobia or an insomnia. . . . But we cannot "cure" the wrong course which the development of a person has taken. We can only assist him in gradually outgrowing his difficulties so that his development may assume a more constructive course. (p. 333)

Intellectual understanding is well described as follows: "Understanding . . . is the key to nothing except further understanding, but in the last analysis, what else is there? All of life is either ignorance or knowledge, there's no third possibility" (Westlake, 1974, p. 157). But in fact, there is a third possibility. Facilitating the patient's move beyond intellectual knowledge of what drives her behavior (though it may start that way) to an emotional aha moment of realization is the very hard work at the core of therapy. Without emotion, the realization, whatever it may be, "has not become real to her; it has not become her personal property; it has not taken roots in her" (Horney, 1950, pp. 342–343). In other words, understanding remains intellectual, as in the expression, *I see, said the blind man.* An aha insight is realization electrified with emotion. By definition, ahas are transformational. In the wake of even a minor emotionally resonant insight, the patient understands herself in a new way, which then allows for choices not possible before.

My patient Sandra's brother Ethan was unreliable, amoral, manipulative, and made Sandra's life miserable. Sandra was aware Ethan was cheating on his wife, neglecting his son (who spent more time with Sandra's family than with his own), and taking advantage of their mother. She also suspected Ethan, as office manager to a large legal practice, was embezzling cash payments. She couldn't quite turn a blind eye to Ethan's character but confronting it was simply too scary. She rationalized, took responsibility for, and cleaned up much of the damage that Ethan inflicted on their extended family.

But when Ethan tried to seduce his wife's sister Jenna (who was disgusted and told Sandra), Sandra couldn't deny the reality any longer. "My brother is just like our father!" Since their father had a long history of contacts with law enforcement for domestic abuse and violence, forgery, and embezzlement, she'd just realized Ethan wasn't merely difficult, but dangerous. In the wake of this aha moment, she withdrew from her enabling role and became more self-protective, choices she wouldn't have made before.

Entitlement claims reflect the false self's focus on the outside world. When the false self's focus is inside oneself, the "tyranny of the should" comes into play. Shoulds, Horney posits, prop up the idealized self with inner dictates—what she *should* be able to do, to be, to feel, to know—and taboos on how she *should not* be. The scope of these demands on the self, though understandable, are too difficult, irrational, and rigid to be met. Despite intellectual awareness of their unreasonable nature, the idealized self disregards the unfeasibil-ity of meeting these expectations (Horney, 1950).

As an example, during my medical school years, especially the first two academic years, despite know-ing better, I tyrannized myself with a persistent irra-tional expectation that *I should know all this already.* Obviously, I didn't. In more rational moments, but still irrationally, I'd hear myself saying, *I should be able to master all this quickly.* Many of my classmates suf-fered from variations on this theme. Asking myself the logical question—*If I should know it all, why am I in training?*—didn't help.

That's because cognitive logic fails to penetrate the irrational core—the psycho-logic—of tyranni-cal shoulds. Depression, anxiety, and other dysphoric affects inevitably follow when the idealized self is con-fronted by undeniable, reality-based evidence. A rigid adherence to these shoulds and denial of the real self's limitations lead inevitably to self-hate, troubled inter-personal relations, and therapy. This is another reason a training analysis, *de rigeur* back in the day, is still worth doing. I found mine immensely helpful in uncov-ering, understanding, and recovering from this kind of nonsense. I became a healthier person for it and, of course, a better therapist.

Relationships Exist in a Social Matrix

Both Winnicott and Sullivan postulated that the interpersonal environment a child is raised within supports or inhibits healthy intrapsychic development, and subsequent interpersonal skills, to various degrees. Winnicott coined the phrase "good enough mother" in 1953 after observing thousands of babies and their mothers. He astutely observed that the difference between good mothers and bad mothers is not the mistakes they make when raising their children but what they do with those errors (Yalom, 2002). It's useful to expand this concept to ourselves as therapists. The difference between being helpful or unhelpful to our patients is not the mistakes we make in session, but what we do with them when they happen.

Being human, naturally I make mistakes with patients. Before I made the blooper that follows, I spent a great deal of energy obsessively second-guessing myself in a doomed attempt to avoid making any. I was in session with Ed, an elderly schizophrenic who had never returned from the psychotic break he'd suffered in his late twenties. Prior to that he'd been a beloved history teacher and popular performing storyteller. He was fortunate: psychiatry's limited range of medications for the treatment of psychosis helped his mood and relatedness, though his delusions remained untouched. He spent most of his sessions entertaining me with jokes, in between which I assessed his mental status, medication compliance, health, support system, and so forth.

He always—every session, for years—asked me if he should get tested for syphilis (part of his delusional system), after which we engaged in a stereotyped exchange that concluded with my saying no, he didn't need to, and him thanking me. The mood in the room that day was relaxed and jovial; we'd done a lot of laughing. Then he said, again referring to getting tested for syphilis, "I was afraid to ask. I didn't want you to think I was crazy."

And here I goofed, for a grin escaped me and out popped: "Come on Ed, we both know you're crazy! That's why you're here." Our eyes locked. He froze, shrank back into the chair, and pulled his head into his shoulders. *I can't believe I said that.* I felt terrible. There was no way he could tolerate being kidded about his illness. Worse, I hadn't answered the question he was really asking, which was, *Do you like me, crazy and all?*

How to regain his trust? Continuing to smile and maintain eye contact, I beamed: "I'm so sorry! I didn't mean to hurt you. You are adorable! I love working with you." I grounded myself in the quality of the session before this awful moment, the strength of our years-long bond, and his sense of humor. I dialed up the warmth and kept twinkling. He gave me a long searching look and melted. "Good one, Doc."

I grinned hugely—*Oh yay! We're okay!*

"Want to hear a joke?" he asked.

"Sure!"

All of this happened in a flash. Why didn't I speak? There wasn't time, and it wasn't necessary. An astounding majority of human communication occurs without words, through facial expression, eye contact, tone of voice, movement, and posture, all functions of the right cerebral hemisphere.

> In order to receive and monitor the patient's non-verbal bodily-based attachment communications, the affectively attuned clinician must shift from constricted left-hemispheric attention that focuses on local detail to more widely expanded right-hemispheric attention that focuses on global detail. . . . In the session, the empathic therapist is consciously explicitly attending to the patient's verbalizations . . . [but] is also listening and interacting at another level, . . . one that implicitly

processes moment-to-moment attachment communications . . . at levels beneath awareness. . . . These
implicit communications are expressed within the
therapeutic alliance between the client's and therapist's right brain systems. (Schore, 2019, pp. 27–28)

(Chapter 3 covers the right and left hemispheres in
more detail.)

Communicating my remorse to Ed with whole-body
expression repaired the breach in our alliance within a
matter of seconds. It's so simple, really. What do we all
want? To be accepted, from soup to nuts—especially
the nuts. How wonderful that Ed forgave me! And how
resilient, trusting, and connected he was, despite his
fragility. He didn't choose his illness, and he remained
disabled despite treatment. We both had to live with
that. I'm competent and full of good will, but still, I'll
occasionally say the wrong thing. We both had to live
with that, too. One mistake and time stopped. We sized
each other up. Ed's psychosis, my insensitive gaffe,
those fell away. We reconnected as human beings, and
once again all was right with the world.

This incident affirmed four things for me. One,
making mistakes is unavoidable. Two, even when my
mistake hurts a patient, that is never my intention.

Three, my commitment to doing no harm reliably guides me when doing damage control. Four, a heart to heart with myself after the fact helps prevent me from making that particular mistake again. I'll move on to make a new one. "An essential relational element of any treatment encounter is how we work with what is being communicated but not symbolized with words" (Schore, 2019, p. 29).

Sullivan's work focused on the role of communication between individuals, and the social matrix embedding those individuals. He saw the psychiatrist's role in the therapy process as that of participant observer, a concept from anthropology and social science in which the researcher/clinician participates in the group's activities while also observing the group's behavior and interactions. Sullivan (1953) posited that, first, much mental disorder results from and is perpetuated by inadequate communication caused by the interference of anxiety: "Anxiety, as a phenomenon of relatively adult life, can often be explained plausibly as anticipated unfavorable appraisal of one's current activity by someone whose opinion is significant" (p. 113). And second, when two people are in relationship, as a patient and therapist are, what they each do and say affects not just each other but their shared community as well.

For the past thirty years, I've lived and practiced in a small rural town (population 23,000), where a clinician faces two realities. First, everyone is connected to everyone, be it through family, work, or friendship. Second, there are too many patients and not enough clinicians, especially in mental health. Handling the boundary and confidentiality issues that arise when treating one or more members of an extended family or friendship circle is an unavoidable challenge (Gitlin, 2019).

I once treated three friends separately but simultaneously, each seeing me for over a decade. Nancy, Tilly, and Gabby had been friends since elementary school. I had no choice but to take on the role of participant observer to their group process for they often used their individual sessions to express worries about each other—a clinical goldmine and confidentiality minefield. Their dynamic with each other, and me, serves as a good example of Sullivan's two postulates, namely that anxiety prevents open communication, and whatever happens between one dyad in a group affects the rest of the group.

When Nancy told me in passing, assuming I knew, that Gabby had suffered from alcoholism in her early twenties, this was news to me. Gabby had lied when I had inquired routinely at our first appointment years before. Nancy continued, saying she feared Gabby had relapsed, "She's denying drinking but I can smell the wine on her breath." When I asked Nancy if she'd be okay with me bringing her concern up with Gabby, she said, "Sure, tell her I told you," Nancy said. "If she gets mad at me, I've got big shoulders."

Gabby was evasive with me, and angry at Nancy for blowing her cover. Of course they told Tilly, who was mad at the two of them for involving me, and at me for holding Gabby's feet to the fire (gently). Thus, their interactions with one another and with me rippled through the treatment group at large. I handled this overtly by having them in for a few group sessions, which they appreciated. There are few things more gratifying to patients than rebonding around giving me hell. Gabby later confessed in her individual session that she was relieved I knew her secret. She hadn't wanted to tell me for fear I would discharge her.

The Here and Now

A foundational premise of our work is that patients come to therapy burdened with the primary anxiety that causes them the suffering they seek relief from. Patients also bring the secondary anxiety of not knowing what to expect from us and the treatment. In individual therapy, group therapy, really any kind of therapy, it is important for therapists to mitigate this secondary anxiety by informing patients fully about therapy—its assumptions and rationale, and what they can do to maximize progress.

This includes going over ground rules, including confidentiality, the need for full disclosure, the importance of dreams, the need for patience, and how to receive here-and-now feedback. I do as Yalom (2002) does, who informs patients this way:

> Sometimes your descriptions may be unintentionally biased, and I've found that I can be more helpful to you by focusing on the one relationship where I have the most accurate information—the relationship between you and me. . . . I shall often ask you to examine what is happening between the two of us. (p. 86)

Yalom incorporated existential reality into the therapy process through an overt and realistic acknowledgment of life's tragic nature. He assumes that patients often fall into despair when confronted with the harsh facts of the human condition. The existential approach posits that the inner conflicts that torment people issue not just from a struggle with suppressed strivings, internalized significant adults, and fragments of forgotten traumatic memories but also from a confrontation with the givens of existence—death, isolation, meaning of life, and freedom (Yalom, 2002). Moreover, therapists are not exempt.

> During my training I was often exposed to the idea of the fully analyzed therapist, but as I have progressed through life, formed intimate relationships with a good many of my therapist colleagues, met the senior figures in the field, been called upon to render help to my former therapists and teachers, and myself become a teacher and an elder, I have come to realize the mythic nature of this idea. We are all in this together and there is no therapist and no person immune to the inherent tragedies of existence. (p. 8)

Or, as musician and creative Frank Zappa put it, *We are all bozos on this bus.* For most of my patients—and probably most people—accepting the absurdity of our understandable yet unobtainable human wish to transcend life's core realities is an ongoing struggle salted with resentment. My patient Sharon, sixty-nine, faced with her husband's slow decline into dementia, acidly observed, "Great. . . . Just what I wanted, another frickin' growth opportunity." The patient's resentment can also target us. My patient Carol, twenty-six, objected to my taking a vacation: "Two weeks?! What about me?"

Yalom (2002) maintains that the paramount task of therapist and patient "is to build a relationship together that will itself become the agent of change" (p. 34). Therefore, nothing is more important to a therapist than the care and maintenance of the relationship to the patient in the here and now of the session.

> The here-and-now refers to the immediate events of the therapeutic hour, to what is happening *here* (in this office, in this relationship, in the in-betweenness—the space between me and you) and *now*; in this immediate hour. It is basically an ahistoric approach and *de-emphasizes* (but does not negate the importance of) the patient's historical past or events of his or her outside life. (p. 46)

The rationale for using the here and now in therapy rests on two assumptions: the importance of interper-

sonal relationships, and the idea of the therapy relationship as a social microcosm. The people important
to us throughout life—our surrounding interpersonal
environment—exert tremendous influence over who
we become. Our self-image develops to a large degree
by how we perceive ourselves to be appraised and
valued by these important figures. Because therapy
is a social microcosm, eventually the patient's interpersonal problems will manifest in the here and now
of the therapy relationship. In other words, patients
will relate to us in the same way that gets them into
trouble with others. When patients bring up a prob-
lematic interaction with another person, our ability
to facilitate their awareness of their contribution to
the problem is limited by having to take their word
for what happened, a view that is frequently inaccu-
rate. Resulting insights tend to stay intellectual rather
than emotional.

However, when patients dysfunctionally interact
with us in the here and now, the work becomes much
more accurate and immediate. This enables us to give
patients feedback right then about how *we* were affected
by their behavior. In turn, patients are more likely to
grasp on an emotional level that what they are doing
in the treatment relationship is generalizable to other,

important relationships in their life (Yalom, 2002). In other words, here-and-now work facilitates the transformation of intellectual understanding into the emotional aha of self-awareness.

When my patient Carol demanded I curtail my vacation plans because she couldn't do without me, she gave me the perfect opening in the here and now of the session to address her entitled dependency: I should put my needs aside for hers, as should her husband and her coworkers.

"I know. I'm so annoying," I said with a rueful smile. "If only I didn't have this vexing need to recharge." She stared at me. I continued, "If only your husband didn't need to travel for his job." I paused, raising my eyebrows. "And, it goes without saying, your coworkers should never get sick, leaving you to cover." She gasped as the insight hit.

"Oh my god!" She covered her face with her hands for a moment before looking up. "I'm so embarrassed. I've been whining like a little kid." She'd grasped the pattern, at the gut level.

"Whine away," I said. "You don't have to like it. But you do have to accept other people have needs too."

"I know." She paused. "But I don't want to!" She

burst out laughing. We went on to have a very
productive session.

Commentary on the here and now is a unique aspect of
the therapeutic relationship. There are few human situations in which we are permitted, much less encouraged,
to comment on the immediate behavior of another. It is
compelling but also risky. Packaging feedback in ways
that patients find acceptable and experience as caring
is a must. Carol and I had worked together for several
years. She had a good sense of humor, and I knew
she could handle a little low-key irony. Yalom (2002)
emphasizes that the words we use matter. If a patient is
boring, for example, she can't take offense if we speak
to how we feel "shut out" or "distanced," how we wish
to feel closer, more connected, and more engaged. Talk
about how you feel, Yalom says, not about what the
patient is doing.

Empathy, Observation, and Process

Psychologist and founding father of psychotherapy
research Carl Rogers identified three essential characteristics of the effective therapist: accurate empathy,
unconditional positive regard, and genuineness. Rog-

ers amassed a considerable body of evidence support-ing the therapeutic effectiveness of empathy. Patients whose therapists enter accurately into their world will profit enormously simply from the experience of being fully seen and fully understood (Yalom, 2002).

We learn best about ourselves and our behavior through personal participation in interaction with others. This is especially true in therapy, for we com-bine observation with analysis. Feedback can focus on *content*—the actual words and concepts expressed—or on *process*, the nature of the relationship between the individuals who express those words and concepts (Yalom, 2002). Yalom has observed that patients become most energized, engaged, and alive when the discussion focuses on process. "People want to interact with others, are excited by giving and receiving feedback, yearn to learn how they are perceived by others, want to slough off their facades and become intimate" (p. 64).

"Effective therapy consists of an alternating sequence: *evocation and experiencing* of affect followed by *analysis and integration* of affect" (p. 71).

•

The doorknob bombshell is one of many ways patients reveal sensitive information, the sharing of which leaves them vulnerable to us clinicians. We build trust by behaving predictably. Maintaining the frame of the session by beginning and ending on time is one concrete way we confirm our dependability. That patients release information at the last minute is not just a function of their trust in us, although the importance of that trust is undeniable. Delivering new material in the teeth of an impending deadline—the end of the session—is also a function of how the brain works.

One Brain, Two Cerebral Hemispheres, Two Minds

The brain is not just a tool for grappling with the world. It is what brings the world about.

— IAN MCGILCHRIST, *The Master and His Emissary: The Divided Brain and the Making of the Western World*

This chapter reviews a few of the differences between the brain's two hemispheres that affect how they work together (or don't) to generate our experience of being alive in the world. Understanding these differences enlarges our understanding of mental processes, enriches our work with our patients, and gives context to the next two chapters. Those chapters describe how the *clinical relationship* between the patient and the clinician mirrors that of the right and left hemispheres, respectively (Chapter 4), and how the *clinical treatment* can be usefully understood as a creative work in progress, cocreated by the patient and clinician in the same way that a writer's right and left hemispheres cocreate a novel (Chapter 5). These two metaphors drive my argument that doorknob moments can be a useful result of consistently ending on time.

Right Versus Left

At the cellular level, the brain

> is a network—a collection of parts that are connected to function as a single unit. You are surely familiar with other networks that surround us. The internet is a network of connected devices. . . . Your social network is a collection of connected people. Your brain, in turn, is a network of 128 billion neurons connected as a single, massive, and flexible structure. (Barrett, 2020, pp. 30–31)

This vast, mind-bogglingly complex neural network of connectivity and plasticity defies our wish to tag specific areas with specific functions. No one neuron has just one function: a single neuron can take on different roles at different times. Any neuron can group with others to do more than one thing. Conversely, different groups of neurons can produce the same result. Some neurons are so flexibly connected that their main job is to have many jobs. Our actions and experiences can be created in multiple ways when the brain is working as a unified whole (Barrett, 2020).

But when the two cerebral hemispheres are separated from each other, the brain is no longer able to function as a single network. Instead, it becomes two networks, two brains, each side going its own way, functioning independently of the other. On the macro level, "split brain" studies done by cognitive neuroscientist Roger Wolcott Sperry and colleagues in the 1970s revealed significant differences in function between the right and left cerebral hemispheres. Sperry's research explored the behavioral and cognitive consequences to individuals whose hemispheres had been surgically separated—"split"—by severing the corpus callosum to treat intractable seizures.

The corpus callosum is the band of neural tissue connecting the two hemispheres at their base, which allows the two hemispheres to communicate with each other. Sperry's studies revealed that each hemisphere, independent of the other, is able to do all an individual needs to live in the world, with the exception of speech. (The speech centers are located on the left side only.)

> Each hemisphere is . . . a conscious system in its own right, perceiving, thinking, remembering, reasoning, willing, and emoting. . . . Both the left and right hemispheres may be conscious simultaneously, in different, even mutually conflicting mental experiences that run along in parallel. (Sperry, 1961, pp. 1749–1757)

Significantly, he also discovered that the corpus callosum's primary purpose is to *inhibit* the two hemispheres from interfering with each other's functioning. In 1981, Sperry and colleagues David H. Hubel and Torsten N. Wiesel were awarded a Nobel Prize in Physiology or Medicine for this split-brain research.

Sperry's experiments studied the two hemispheres artificially separated from each other. But the two hemispheres are interconnected in the normal brain and work together most of the time. In fact, nothing the normal brain does is confined entirely to one hemisphere or the other. For example, while the speech centers located only in the left contain the dictionary and syntax we use to speak, the right side is able to read, understand language, and perform language functions that the left hemisphere cannot, such as poetry, metaphor, irony, and humor.

At any one time, for any activity and mental process, both hemispheres will be actively involved at the cellular level. Brain organization varies across individuals— concepts of right and left function are *not* universal. While the differences are real, they are not absolute: generalizations are just that, generalizations, not rules (McGilchrist, 2009). Yet that does not exclude that the two hemispheres may have radically different agendas. Studies over long periods of time with large numbers of individuals make it apparent that each hemisphere initiates a way of being in the world that is in conflict with the other (McGilchrist, 2009). We've all felt pulled in opposing directions when making a decision, as if we have two minds. Well . . . we *do* have two minds. Moreover, we've known this intuitively for a very long time:

> This way, that way
> I do not know
> what to do: I
> am of two minds.

> — SAPPHO (630–570 BC),
> *Sappho: A New Translation* (1986)

The world we actually experience at any point in time is determined on the macro level by which hemisphere's version of the world dominates, for the two sides appear to differ profoundly in mode of functioning, strengths, limitations, and world view. They represent two individually coherent but incompatible aspects of the world. There is evidence that as individuals, we consistently prefer using one hemisphere over the other when engaged in particular activities. However, those differences between individuals tend to generalize to one preference in large groups (McGilchrist, 2009). McGilchrist explicates the following durable generalizations about how each hemisphere attends to and experiences the reality of the outside world.

The right hemisphere lives in a world in which everything is new, nothing is repeated, and nothing can ever be "known," because there is no past—there is only the now.

> No man ever steps in the same river twice,
> for it is not the same river and he is not the
> same man.
>
> — HERACLITUS (CA. 500 BC)

The left fixes experience into a series of static, separate points, which give the illusion of continuity in the way separate frames of a film speeding by give the illusion of movement.

The right hemisphere deals with a thing as a whole within its context, as a gestalt. "Gestalt" is defined by *Merriam-Webster's Collegiate Dictionary* as "something that is made of many parts and yet is somehow more than or different from the combination of its parts." For example, we take in—comprehend—the humor of a cartoon all at once, as an aha or gestalt, and we burst out laughing. Trying to explain why it's funny to someone who doesn't get it rarely works because explaining is a left-hemisphere function.

The left hemisphere understands a thing by removing it from its context and then breaking it down into its component parts. It groups these separate elements into classes, from which predictions can be made, which is its source of power in the world. The "whole" the left reconstructs from these parts will be very different from the whole made by the right hemisphere, just as a written clinical summary of a session with a patient can never reflect the whole person we engage with in that session.

The right hemisphere's focus is broad. Widely networked with the left hemisphere, the right processes experience through bodily sensation and sensory input—visual, auditory, touch, taste, smell, and kinesthetic awareness of the body in space. It interfaces directly with the external environment and is comfort-able with uncertainty, and with what it doesn't know or recognize—in other words, new data. It is the first responder when action is needed, and it tells you what to do *without words*—your hand has already pulled away from a hot burner by the time your left hemi-sphere thinks, *Hot!*

The right hemisphere lives concretely, in an unbroken stream of moments, always in the present, processing experience in time as an ongoing narrative. It is creative and sources without "formal" instruction the first draft of all narrative structures—those with a beginning, middle, and end—that we present to the outside world. These include first drafts of stories, drawings, choreog-raphies, songs, scientific experiments, anything with a narrative arc. Somehow, it "knows" what to do and does it before the conscious self "decides." This is how young children draw complex images without a plan.

The right hemisphere takes in images—art, car-toons, paintings, drawings—all at once, in one gulp, as an aha moment. The right *thinks in images.* And since it is at the front line, interfacing directly with external reality, our first "thoughts" are actually images and/or sensations, which carry with them a profound and full understanding of what is happening, though that understanding may remain implicit and inarticulate. This happens all the time and everywhere, of course, as happened with me in the following treatment.

> My chronically suicidal, dysthymic patient Phillip, fifty-eight and divorced, had been in treatment with me for over twenty-five years with very little "improve-ment." As the years rolled on, and nothing essential changed in Phillip's experience of his world, I consulted colleagues. I took courses to expand my skill set. I referred him for expert second opinions. Phillip continued to suffer without respite.
>
> Seeing his name on my day's schedule began to fill me with dread, a dread that I endured far too long without examination.

Noticing I was bored led, in a way that I can't articulate, to this insight. Why? And just like that, I was excited and curious about Phillip and his treatment once again. Only the right hemisphere can bring us information that we don't already know and think thoughts we have never thought before.

The left hemisphere deals only with what it is familiar—what it has encountered before—and the world it has made for itself. It is heavily interconnected within itself, much less so globally. This facilitates its primary strength—narrow focus—but also reflects on a neural level the self referring way it operates. The left hemisphere is analytic, critical, and logical. It revises and polishes the first drafts the right generates.

When the right hemisphere engages with the outside world, it transfers undifferentiated sensory information to the left for processing. The left hemisphere, like an owl closing in on a mouse with claws outstretched, focuses in on *what it recognizes* within the novelty, ambiguity, and complexity of what the right hemisphere has sent it. It translates that into words, bringing that translation into consciousness. This happens so quickly that even as your right hemisphere jerks your hand away from that hot burner, your left thinks it got there first when it yells, *Hot!*

This suggests that the left hemisphere is mostly unaware of the right and thinks (mistakenly) it is making first contact with new information. Because its voice is loud and verbal, we hear it in our heads, consciously, which leads to us to draw the same, mistaken conclusion—we think those words reflect something new. But they don't—they reflect only what the left hemisphere has seen before. The left hemisphere is incapable of creating anything new.

And, because it catalogs time as a series of disconnected, static points, the left hemisphere cannot follow or produce a narrative arc—something with a beginning, middle, and end. The qualities that enable the left to edit, revise, and polish are also what make it critical, bossy, self-conscious, and resistant to change. It's the source of that loud, know-it-all, nasty inner voice creative people call The Critic. (More on the left's contribution to the creative process in Chapter 4.)

Certainty is related to narrowness. The more certain we are of something, the less we "see." The fovea of the eye, a tiny region in the retina at the center of gaze, can see with one hundred times the resolution of peripheral vision. But, with that resolution, it perceives only a sliver of the entire visual field (McGilchrist, 2009). Denial, a left hemisphere specialty, works in a similar way, focusing narrowly on one thing, or a few, while ignoring everything else—the context. The left's ability to exclude relevant or unrecognized data is associated with decreased self-awareness and unrealistically optimistic mood—the left hemisphere is always a winner. Right-hemisphere deficits, such as sociopathy or damage caused by trauma or stroke, leaves the person "crippled by naively optimistic forecasting of outcomes" (McGilchrist, 2009, p. 85).

The right hemisphere's tendency to depression and sorrow makes it more realistic in assessing others and ourselves. It is not that insight makes us depressed, McGilchrist (2009) suggests, but that depression gives us insight, thus allowing us to strongly connect with and have empathy for others. The more connected we are, the more we are likely to suffer and the more likely we are to feel shame, guilt, and responsibility for others. Sociopaths, with their right hemisphere deficits, are incapable of empathic interpersonal connection—they cannot love another or receive love (Stout, 2006).

The frontal lobes of the two cerebral hemispheres manage competing needs, with the help of the corpus callosum, which inhibits them from interfering with each other. The left's world is about "me" and "my needs," which includes manipulating the world for "my benefit." This is an attitude of targeted attention, with a grasping energy that doesn't want to let go and that reduces interactions to transactions. For example, a man paying a woman to have sex with him is engaging in a transaction. Paying for his orgasm is the man's only concession to the needs of the woman providing the service.

By contrast, the right hemisphere keeps an open and wide attention on the surrounding context, in order, for example, to maintain a hovering lookout for danger. It is oriented to the world "at large," beyond the self, but that includes "me *in relation to* others." This is a receptive attention, with diffuse alertness to allegiances outside oneself. For example, when a couple makes love, that is an interaction within the context of relationship and interpersonal connection.

To maintain the viability of their relationship, each person balances personal needs with the needs of their partner. The right hemisphere checks the left's natural impulse toward selfishness and is the source of self-control and the power to resist temptation. The right is responsible for "almost every aspect of the development of mental functioning in early childhood and the self as a social, empathic being" (McGilchrist, 2009, p. 86).

When we are ill, we often temporarily withdraw from our relationships and outside interests. I've noticed that when patients are caught up in their suffering, they don't notice office décor—most of their attention is directed inside. What little attention they focus on me is driven by how much (or how little) I am helping them. When a patient asks me if a pottery bowl on an end table (that has been there all along) is new, I take that interest in their surroundings as a sign they are feeling better. They have started to reconnect with the world outside themselves, and with me.

The Right Hemisphere Should Rule but Often Doesn't

The right is responsible for all types of attention except focused attention, the purview of the left. Additionally, the right hemisphere is able to use the left's preferred style, as well as its own (McGilchrist, 2009). When attention is divided, the right, with its greater flexibility, can and should take the primary role, guiding the left's local attention within the larger context. In an ideal world, the left would readily return information it has processed to the right hemisphere.

But in real life, the left hemisphere resists doing so because of allostasis. *Allostasis* is the brain's ability to automatically predict and prepare to meet the body's needs *before they arise* (Barrett, 2020). The left deals with what it knows and prioritizes what it expects—its process is predictive. It is efficient in routine situations where things are predictable. Therefore, it is drawn by its expectations. When prediction is difficult, as when needing to rethink initial assumptions, the right hemisphere outperforms the left (McGilchrist, 2009). However, prediction, even if faulty, saves energy and resources. All too often, a problem better solved by the right hemisphere gets badly solved by the left. When that problem crops up again, the left recognizes it and solves it again simply because that is what it did before, which saves energy. When it comes to bodily (and brain) energy budgeting, prediction beats reaction (Barrett, 2020). What exists tends to persist.

In this way the left hemisphere, which should be subordinate to the right, tends to acquire and hang on to excessive power. On the interpersonal and social levels, this is probably one reason that abusive marriages and systems of institutional oppression keep going—the energy required to change them is far greater than that needed to maintain them. That can happen in therapy, too.

There I sat with Phillip in session, finally aware that I hadn't had a new insight or felt alive in this treatment for a very long time. My left hemisphere had taken over; I had been behaving automatically instead of thoughtfully; and I was stuck. Logical conclusion: the treatment was becalmed, like a sailboat without a breeze. I needed Phillip to give me something new to work with. Yet self-disclosure is always risky for a patient, and I didn't know how to support him in taking that leap of faith.

Then the catalytic event occurred. (It's been my recurring experience that when I am out of ideas, patients generously help me out.) Phillip called me during office hours in a rage. He'd received a letter from his insurance company that I'd stopped taking his coverage, which I hadn't. He rejected all reassurance that I'd fix it, canceled his next appointment, and hung up on me.

He paged me that same night, after midnight, startling me awake. My heart raced—had he become suicidal? No. He ranted about the insurance! I went from fearful to flabbergasted to furious. "This is not an emergency," I finally snapped. "I'm not talking to you now." I ended the call as he was speaking.

I'd lost my temper. I was horrified. A core principle from our training states that sharing intense negative emotion with a patient is at best clinically ill advised, at worst harmful. I tossed and turned the rest of the night, kept awake by a scatter of worries and speculations.

As months went by and Phillip didn't call, I see-sawed between two opposing assessments about how I'd handled him. I didn't question my anger, which was legitimate. After all, he'd taken advantage by using the emergency pager to berate me, instead of keeping his appointment. Plus, it was unreason-able to expect myself to be as skillful when awakened at midnight as I was during the workday.

Still, I faulted my delivery. Phillip was a troubled patient in a lot of pain, and I shouldn't have lost patience. He'd frequently angered me in the past, but I'd never before lost my grip. What was different this time? (This is always a great question to ask when something goes "awry" in the treatment.)

Over the years, whenever something cropped up over which I had no control, Phillip's knee jerk reaction was to accuse me of malice—I'd done it, whatever it was, to him on purpose. In parallel knee-jerk, I worked hard to convince him that of course I hadn't. This paging incident, while more extreme, ran true to form. As I considered this history, my mind lit up: like the controlling player in a tennis match, Phillip had me running all over the court to prove I was trustworthy.

In a flash, this image made obvious two powerful aspects of our dynamic. First, *I* was supposed to be running *him,* not the other way around. Second, *he wasn't mad about the insurance.* He was mad that *I wasn't doing my job.* I was supposed to be guiding the treatment, but instead, he was. *I had let him down.* No wonder the treatment had come to a standstill.

This image and its metaphorical message arrived simultaneously—an aha moment without words and with full comprehension. This is how the right hemisphere thinks and communicates. We carry out most mental processes that we consider "thinking" outside of consciousness and without words. We make sense of the world, form categories and concepts, weigh and evaluate decisions, and solve problems, all without language.

> The words or language, as they are written or spoken, do not seem to play any role in the mechanism of my thought.
>
> — ALBERT EINSTEIN

In his seminal work *Visual Thinking,* Rudolph Anheim notes that perceptual and pictoral shapes aren't just translations of thought: they are the origins of thoughts themselves (Arnheim, 1969). The right hemisphere mediates nonverbal communication and music, along with most forms of imagination or innovation—intuitive problem solving, spiritual thinking, and artistic creativity (McGilchrist, 2009). An astonishing 80% of human communication occurs *nonverbally.* Before we learn to speak, we communicate with our primary caretakers and others by touch, eye contact, and all the vocalizations that we use to sing: pitch, tone, phrasing, rhythm, volume, and more. Think of the chef's kiss gesture—it says so much without words by delivering its meaning with the whole self: mouth making the smooch sound, facial expression, hand gesture, stance, attitude.

Now that I had grasped what Phillip was angry about, many of his behavioral communications—irritated tone of voice, constant criticism and fault finding, canceling his appointment, paging me when he didn't have an emergency—made sense. On the process level, he'd paged because, from his point of view, it *was* an emergency. (Not that he knew consciously; I'm sure he didn't.) My "getting" these nonverbals for what they meant changed everything. And notice that I didn't logic out this understanding. The realization came to me fully formed when I "saw" us playing tennis.

Attention Is a Relationship

By concerning itself with *what* a thing is and removing it from its context, the left hemisphere strips that thing of life by reducing it to its parts. Medical training, for example, is heavily dominated by the left hemisphere's preference for the mechanical. We learn to diagnose and treat a specific body part separate from its larger context, the person. A patient in a hospital setting may be referred to as "the liver in Room 302" or "the schizo-phrenic on Ward 9." The left hemisphere breaks down a living being to its components, while the right concerns itself with the person as a unique whole that cannot be reduced to its parts.

The benefit of the left hemisphere's way of isolat-ing things from their context is that it enables us to step away from the overwhelming immediacy of experience—the right hemisphere's engagement with the always changing real world outside of us—allowing us to focus on a particular aspect of reality and how it can be grasped and controlled. This allows us to plan, to solve specific problems, and to take con-trol of our environment rather than simply respond-ing reactively. What is lost, though, is the context—the picture as a whole and whatever is implicit or unartic-ulated, whatever cannot be focused or fixed in place (McGilchrist, 2009).

What the left hemisphere recognizes from the right's transfer of undifferentiated information, it adds to itself in the manner of $1 + 1 = 2$. Not so the right hemisphere. The right organically integrates information the left sends *into* itself, *creating a new whole* in the way a seed incorporates nutrients to grow a stem, and the stem grows leaves, puts out flowers, and bears fruit. That integration can carry with it a sudden and powerful feeling of wonder and awe—an aha moment. When you have such a gestalt experience, there is no turning back from the new understanding—the change is structural and permanent. You can't unfry an egg.

Thus, the right and left hemispheres' ways of being in the world are fundamentally, asymmetrically opposed. They are not equivalent or separate poles. The left concerns itself with *what* a thing is and how it can be used. The right engages with *how* a thing is—its mode of being. These are not different ways of thinking *about* the world—they are different ways of *being* in the world (McGilchrist, 2009). Together, these two ways of being create our *experience of being alive*.

The most important difference between the two hemispheres is the kind of attention each gives to the world—the interaction between our mind-brain and what exists in the world. "Every individual mind is a process of interaction with whatever it is that exists apart from ourselves *according to its own private history* [emphasis mine]" (McGilchrist, 2009, p. 20). In other words, what we notice—bring into being—is influenced by who we are at that moment and what we bring with that attention. "The tree which moves some to tears of joy is in the eyes of others only a green thing that stands in the way" (Blake, 1977, p. 136).

Perhaps this is why "chemistry"—an immediate feeling of mutual compatibility—is a necessary component of the viable client–clinician relationship in treatment (and, really, in any intimate dyad). There is no neutrality. Everything we "know" carries certain beliefs and feelings we've accumulated over time (McGilchrist, 2009). Being a good therapist is not about being neutral and objective, as is often portrayed in fiction and film. It is actually about being present to where you stop and the other person begins, and acquiring the self-control and skill to use that self-awareness in the service of the patient. That's why, if you are a trainee, a training analysis—being in therapy while you are simultaneously learning how to be a therapist—is such a worthwhile experience.

I went into psychiatry to become a therapist who also prescribes. My residency adviser gave me a couple of referrals for well-regarded training analysts, which I followed up. From the moment I walked into her office and made eye contact, I didn't like the first analyst I interviewed. I can't say why beyond a bad feeling, which persisted to the end of the session. When she gave me a follow-up appointment, without asking if I wanted one, I felt too vulnerable to tell her I wasn't coming back. Unfortunately, she picked up the phone when I called to cancel, thwarting my craven wish to leave a message. She was displeased I didn't want to work with her and gratuitously interpreted my decision as resistance. When I hung up, I burst into tears. "The hell with her," said my husband Kevin, also a psych resident, rubbing my back as I sobbed. "She's not for you." Conversely, from the moment I walked into her office and made eye contact with my analyst Robin, I knew she was the one. How did I know? I can't say, but I wasn't wrong. It's a kind of magic. I've enjoyed the reverse experience, too, of knowing immediately that a patient and I would work well together.

The kind of attention we bring to bear on anything influences what we find, along with how we feel about it. In that way, attention is bound up with values. Attention is intrinsically a relationship, not a stand-alone fact. It is an aspect of consciousness itself. Attempting to detach our attention only yields consequences related to that detachment. You can't strip a thing of its context because no context is a context, too (McGilchrist, 2009).

Attention changes what kind of thing comes into being for us: in that way [our attention] changes the world. . . . You would feel changed if I changed the type of my attention. And yet, nothing objectively has changed. . . . So it is . . . with everything . . . we come into contact with. A mountain is a landmark to a navigator, a source of wealth to a prospector. (p. 28)

Phillip returned to treatment after a few months away. Why? He said, "At least you listen." I was amazed—this was the first time, in over two decades of treatment, that he'd acknowledged that I mattered to him. Paradoxically, that I lost my temper sent him the message that *he* mattered to *me*. Interpretating that for him revitalized our connection and the treatment.

Don't think that his overall misery abated or that he stopped challenging my trustworthiness. Just last week, he started up. But all it took to move him from accusing to musing was referencing what we now call The Midnight Page, the iconic example of his interpersonal struggles. Even as Phillip insists he wants to stop assuming the worst of me (and others), change is hard and he continues, unconsciously, attempting to seduce me into colluding

> dysfunctionally as I had before. But those days are
> over—there is no going back from my aha moment.
> The nature of my attention on him had changed,
> which changed our dynamic.

The difference between the right and left hemispheres goes beyond a mere information processing system—it tells us something about the nature of reality and about the nature of our experience of the world. This is easiest to see engaging with our impaired patients and loved ones. Their experience is not just a matter of data loss. "Their world itself has changed" (McGilchrist, 2009, p. 30). That change can be so radical that the nature of our relationship changes, too.

> When he was nineteen, my patient Karen's brother
> Wayne suffered a first break psychotic episode, the
> beginning of the life-long schizophrenia that robbed
> him of his potential and future. When he was twenty-
> two, Karen and her husband Josh visited him at the
> state psychiatric hospital where he was institutional-
> ized. (That was in the early 1980s; those days of long-
> term institutional treatment are over.)
>
> Forty years later, this is the eye-opening and heart-
> breaking exchange she recalled from that visit.

"Wayne," she had asked, "what do you do all day?"

"Oh. . . . I don't know . . . ," he'd said, shaking his head. "I spend all day . . . trying to figure out what's real and . . . what's not real."

Karen said she and her husband were gob-smacked by the devastating acuity of his answer, even as he suffered active delusions, auditory hallucinations, and paranoia.

She told me that recently she'd asked Wayne if he remembered that visit. "Oh yeah," he told her with a grin of pleasure, "Josh gave me $20 for cigarettes." He didn't remember Karen asking him what he did all day. Karen didn't remember that Josh had given him $20 for cigarettes.

Memories are not static and fixed. We don't store them in our brains like files in a computer. The brain reconstructs memories on demand at the cellular level, a process we call "remembering" but is more accurately described as assembling. Moreover, our brain doesn't necessarily use the same neurons to assemble a memory each time we remember it. It may use a different collection entirely (Barrett, 2020). Especially when they are emotionally charged, it pays to remember (ha) that memories shape-shift more than we like to admit, in clinical work as well as in personal life.

Karen tells me Wayne's memories of their shared childhood remain intact. He enjoys waxing nostalgic and in accurate detail about that time, when he was himself. But after the illness took him, his internal world changed, and in direct consequence, so did their relationship. That sense of personal narrative, with the continuity and emotional engagement that memorable events carry, has been mostly absent from his conversation since he became psychotic, she reports, though not completely absent. This makes sense, given that the right frontal cortex sources our sense of a personal "interior" and our sense of self with a history, along with our personal and emotional memory (McGilchrist, 2009).

Classic symptoms of schizophrenia include being socially withdrawn, poorly related, internally preoccupied by auditory hallucinations, and paranoid. Patients deny or, more accurately, lack insight into their illness. These are all signs that the right hemisphere is compromised, leaving the left hemisphere dominant. Medication helps a little, but schizophrenia is profoundly disabling cognitively, emotionally, and especially interpersonally and socially.

And yet, Karen tells me, there are times when the symptoms recede, and her brother is present as himself. For a few precious moments, they connect and are together once more, right hemisphere to right hemisphere. "That always makes me cry," she says. "It reminds me of who he was and how much I miss him."

The Right Hemisphere and Psychotherapy

The right hemisphere is dominant in nonverbal communication, subjective emotional experiences, social relatedness, and implicit learning. Thus, right-brain processes are dominant in psychotherapy. The implicit communication of emotion between the right brains of the patient–therapist dyad, like the infant-mother dyad, has been described as "intersubjectivity." "The right hemisphere, particularly the right frontal region, under normal circumstances plays a crucial role in establishing the appropriate relationship between the self and the world" (Schore, 2019, p. 26).

There is consensus that deficits in these right-brain relational processes result in affective dysregulation. All models of therapeutic intervention share the common goal of improving the effectiveness of emotional self-regulation. At every stage of life, psychotherapy can facilitate the intrinsic plasticity of the patient's right brain (Schore, 2019).

Right-brain creativity appears to be a fundamental aspect of clinical expertise as well.

> [It] is an essential contributor to treatment, both in establishing and maintaining the therapeutic alliance and in reestablishing it after ruptures. . . . [The therapist's right brain] creatively provides a novel relational experience via the therapist's co-participation in interactive repair and regulation of the patient's affective states. (p. 178)

CHAPTER 4

The Power of the Deadline

Therapy as a Creative Process

Philip Roth was asked about his writing
process. In response he said, "The book unfolds
as I write it and reveals itself to me. I discover
what it will be as it comes to life." The same
is true for therapy—it is a story cowritten,
moment by moment with your clients.

— LOUIS COZOLINO, *The Development of
a Therapist: Healing Others–Healing Self*

A viable treatment needs to strike a balance between
predictability, which supports security and reduces
anxiety, and novelty, which promotes learning and
growth but can be unsettling and anxiety provoking. Professional creatives—writers, musicians, sci-
entists, choreographers, cartoonists—have figured
out how to navigate the space between predictability
and novelty that allows them to consistently produce

new work. Interestingly, this has to do with how the brain works.

Only the Right Hemisphere Creates

> The two opposing views of human nature represent the primary motives of each of the two hemispheres of the human brain. At a conscious level, the left side of the brain concerns itself primarily with power motives, while the right side of the brain is steeped in affiliation drives. Only one perspective can press forward into consciousness at a time, and as this occurs, the other perspective recedes into the background.
>
> — ALLAN N. SCHORE, *Right Brain Psychotherapy*

All strategies used by professional creatives enable the right hemisphere to come forward and the cacophony and narrow focus of the left's understanding to recede. To know something consciously—to be aware of it— requires memory. Thus, what the conscious left hemisphere "knows" is already in the past, no longer alive but "re-presented." It isn't possible to "think" your way into something new. As Carl Jung said, "All cognition is akin to recognition" (quoted in McGilchrist, 2009, p. 164).

The right hemisphere relates to others and the world with empathy and intersubjectivity as its ground of consciousness while maintaining an open, patient attention, as opposed to the willful, grasping attention of the left. The right emphasizes process rather than stasis—the journey is more important than the arrival. Creativity and creating are an unveiling rather than a deliberate construction. Perception is primary—the body is the ground of reality and ideas. The emphasis is on uniqueness and on value independent of utility (McGilchrist, 2009).

Mary Parker Follett, in *Creative Experience* (1928) writes, "Concepts can never be presented to me merely, they must be knitted into the structure of my being, and this can only be done through my own activity" (quoted in Barry, 2014, p. 72). Creative work and ideas emerge from bodily experience.

> I [could] never get to the essential core of movement and dance through a cerebral process. I could prepare, order, organize, structure, and edit my creativity in my head, but I couldn't think my way into a dance. To generate ideas, I had to move. You can't

imagine the work, you can only generate ideas when you put pencil to paper, brush to canvas—when you actually do something physical. (Tharp, 2003, p. 99)

Cartoonist, professor, and MacArthur genius grant recipient Lynda Barry (2014) concurs: "The only way to understanding . . . is by making things. Thinking about it, theorizing about it, chatting about it will not get you there" (Barry, 2014, p. 72).

Barry (2014) teaches a daily diary practice that lets us access the right hemisphere's way of engaging with the world. "I think of the comp book as a place for the back of the mind to come forward" (p. 62). The daily diary uses one page in a comp book—the cheap kind with the black-and-white–squiggled cardboard cover—and takes six minutes: in the first two minutes list seven things you *did* yesterday; next two minutes, list seven things you *saw* yesterday; then one minute to write down something you *overheard* yesterday, and one minute to ask yourself a question. That's it. (If you want a longer workout, set a timer for nine minutes, pick one thing you've just listed, and free-write without stopping until the timer dings. You will be amazed to find you've generated a short piece with a narrative arc. More on this in the following pages.)

For maximum benefit, use the original "digital device"—your hand—to write. Don't mull, just list, quickly, the first things that come to mind, without judgment. Nothing is too small or too trivial. For example, the other day, when I rolled the garbage can down the driveway to the curb, I noticed a broken eggshell half, tiny and sky blue, on the grass just beside the asphalt. *Robin's egg?* I asked myself. It went in my daily diary the next day.

> Your daily diary will teach you to hear, see, and remember the world around you. What goes into your diary are *things that you noticed when you became present* [emphasis mine], that is to say when the hamster wheel of thoughts and plans and worries stopped long enough for you to notice where you were and what was going on around you. (Barry, 2014, p. 61)

How is this relevant to working with patients? Anything we do regularly that keeps us present to what we notice helps us with patients. In session, noticing what we notice about the patient, and what is simultaneously going through our minds, without an agenda or judgment, of them or ourselves, is the mindset that enables creative responses to the unexpected. And doorknob bombshells are always unexpected.

Barry gives a five-day workshop called "Writing the Unthinkable" at Omega Institute in Rhinebeck, New York, which I was extremely fortunate to attend several times. With her random-prompt/timed-writing method, it is possible to reliably produce first drafts— *new* work—of any kind *without formal training*. Before I took the workshop, I had never written fiction or drawn cartoons. Not only did Barry teach that it is possible to create a story with a beginning, middle, and end *from scratch* in minutes, but she showed that *it is easy*. All you need is a random prompt—anything from your daily diary lists will work—a timer, and the determination to ignore the left hemisphere's nattering. This is not to say that what emerges will be "good." The point is that something reliably comes alive and is born.

Barry would give us a prompt, set the timer on her phone (which we couldn't see) and we'd go. There was a vague sense of time passing rapidly, along with an urgency to get every word down before it ran out. To hear Barry instructing us to wrap up just before the timer *ding*ed felt as if I were surfacing from an alternate reality. Then she'd ask for a volunteer to read as the rest of us listened while drawing tight spirals on paper. (I suspect drawing those spirals kept our left hemispheres busy, so that we could listen without judgment to what we were hearing.) Barry always knelt beside the reading person's desk, and when they finished, all she said was, "Good. Good." For five days, I was astonished: all the stories I heard, all *my* stories, had a narrative arc—a beginning, a middle, and an end.

I was even more astonished at how vulnerable I felt after reading a raw first draft to the class. When I finished, I couldn't look up from the page. Barry waited me out, and when I finally raised my eyes, there were hers, looking directly into mine with loving kindness. She knew, she'd been there, she didn't have to say a word. Then she said, "Good. Good," and I teared up. Perhaps this is how patients feel with us: raw, exposed, and fragile, dreading rejection yet hoping for affirmation, moved to tears to find us right there.

Here is something my right hemisphere handwrote in twelve pell-mell minutes after briefly studying this random prompt: a black-and-white photo of a toddler standing in a baby walker looking up laughing, something metallic and machine-like in the shadowy background.

You have dropped in to see your uncle who is a butcher at the commercial kitchen he works at. You've just come off duty working the night shift—you're a nurse—and have picked up your daughter Mandy, aged 14 months, from home. Your husband has to go to work. He's gotten her fed, dressed in a long sleeved, long legged onesie, and handed her off to you with a kiss for both of you. You take her in your arms and she smells delightfully of baby, sleep, freshly laundered onesie, soap, and the top of her downy head—that special indescribable smell. You're much too hopped up from work to stay home and so you've taken this little jaunt to Donalli Brothers Meats to see Uncle Vinny. The sun is bright this late spring day and entering the commercial kitchen, it's dark for a moment. You pause, Mandy in one arm, her rolling walker in the other, to get your bearings. Metal doors bang, things clank, there's the sounds of boxes shoved along the linoleum floor. As your eyes adjust, the smell of raw meat, specifically pork, rises slowly through the other food smells, spices, grease, potatoes. "Carol!" you hear a gravelly voice call from across the room, and while your eyes focus, Mandy turns and reaches her arms out to the voice, cooing. "Hi! Uncle Vinny," you say, and walk toward him. "I'm getting ready to grind burger," he says, pointing to a massive pile of red chuck in a 3-foot high bowl that's sitting on the commercial 6-foot long table he's standing by. "Put the baby here, beside the grinder, so she can watch." You do it, and he starts tossing chunks of meat into the funnel of the grinder, a 6-foot tall metal thing with a humongous metal bowl parked at the base—a Kitchen Aid mix master on steroids. Pink curly cues of meat start plopping out in clumps, hitting the bottom of the giant bowl with thumps. Mandy laughs, and Vinny makes googly-eyed faces at her, tossing meat over his head like a juggler, so it flies down in front of her face as it hits the bowl. She crows with delight, hands clasped on the rim of her walker.

I stressed as one word after the other poured from my pen, and no wonder: I was in unknown territory without a map. I had to actively ignore the nagging unease that I didn't know what I was doing, what I was writing didn't make sense, that I was making grammatical errors, that it wasn't any good, blah, blah, blah. The left hemisphere is a killjoy, always finding fault with *what it doesn't recognize*.

But—*tick tock*—I didn't have time deal with that. When the timer buzzed, I squeezed in a few more words and that was it. Done. I had *no idea what I'd just created*. Imagine my surprise to find I'd come up with a coherent narrative from who-knows-where. I'd started the process saying, just like one of Barry's cartoon characters: *"But . . . I don't know how. . . .* Yet, her pencil—and my pen—answered: *It turns out you do"* (Barry, 2014, p. 94).

The random prompt stimulates memory and imagination. The timer imposes a terminal endpoint, aka a deadline. Could it be that the pressure of writing *without stopping* (while ignoring the left hemisphere's demands to backtrack, correct, delete, improve) within a background awareness that time is passing, soon to run out, supports the right hemisphere in getting the job done? What is that job? Perhaps it is as simple as creating and closing the narrative arc, whatever the format, within a specific time period. Quality control is the left hemisphere's job, but only after the right has finished.

> I don't need time. I need a deadline.
>
> — DUKE ELLINGTON

There appears to be a loose consensus among professional creatives that constraints enable and support creative output. Jazz pianist, song writer, and prolific composer Duke Ellington wrote or collaborated on more than one thousand compositions; his body of work is the largest recorded personal jazz legacy. He was awarded a posthumous Pulitzer Prize Special Award in 1999. Clearly, deadlines worked for him.

As they do for dancer and choreographer Twyla Tharp:

> Limits are a secret blessing, and bounty can be a curse. I've been on enough big-budget film sets to appreciate the malignant influence of abundance and bloat. . . . No deprivation, no inspiration. . . . Time, for example, is our most limited resource, but it is not the enemy of creativity that we think it is. The ticking clock is our friend if it gets us moving with urgency and passion. Give me a writer who thinks he has all the time in the world and I'll show you a writer who never delivers. . . . Necessity will continue to be the mother of invention. (Tharp, 2003, pp. 124–126)

And poet Robert Frost is described as feeling similarly: "According to Frost, 'the self-imposed restrictions of meter in form' . . . work to a poet's advantage; they liberate him" (Poetry Foundation, 2016, n.p.).

A new idea, insight, or awareness comes from the right hemisphere as three-dimensional sensation and image, carrying with it a sense of full comprehension. Writing, controlled by the left hemisphere, "is linear and sequential; Sentence B must follow Sentence A, and Sentence C must follow Sentence B, and eventually you get to Sentence Z. The hard part of writing isn't the writing; it's the thinking" (Zinsser, 2009). Speaking coherently and writing accessibly require our left hemispheres to find something it can pull out and explicate in this mechanistic way from the amorphous implicit offering of the right. The resulting product is so narrow and limited compared to the right's aha of understanding that frustration is a writer's constant companion. Novelist Ann Patchett (2013) describes this eloquently:

> I make up a novel in my head. . . . This is the happiest time in the arc of my writing process. . . . This book I have not yet written one word of is a thing of indescribable beauty. . . . All I have to do is put it down on paper. . . . When I can't think of another stall, when putting it off has actually become more painful than doing it [when the right's persistence finally overcomes the left's resistance] . . . I take [it] from . . . my head and I press it down against my desk, and there, with my own hand, I kill it. It's not that I want to kill it, but it's the only way I can get

something that is so three dimensional onto the flat page. . . . Imagine running over a butterfly with an SUV. Everything that was beautiful about this living thing—all the color, the light and movement—is gone. What I'm left with is the dry husk of my friend, the broken body chipped, dismantled, and poorly assembled. Dead. That's my book. . . . The journey from the head to hand is perilous and lined with bodies. (pp. 24–25)

Notice Patchett's use of multisensory metaphors to kindle our imagination, understand the task's difficulty, and empathize with the emotional determination such an undertaking requires. Only a few are willing, she says, to trade in "the living beauty of imagination for the stark disappointment of words" (p. 25). Barry (2014) is more sanguine: "Project paralysis will pass! It cannot be avoided! For a little while you'll be scared to begin! And then . . . " (p. 190) you begin, you become absorbed, and the fear disappears.

The linearity of written language makes reading hard, too. We are forced to take in one word at a time and build comprehension that way, like placing bricks to make a wall. Especially when reading nonfiction, the experience can be arduous, time-consuming, and decontextualized—barren of emotional or visceral experience. Using language that kindles images, sensation, and imagination mitigates this linearity by accessing the reader's right hemisphere's three-dimensional bodily experience of reality.

The right hemisphere can also hold several ambiguous possibilities simultaneously without premature closure on the outcome. This tolerance of uncertainty is required for all nonlinear uses of language—metaphor, humor, irony, and poetry (McGilchrist, 2009). These allow meaning to be taken in like an image: all at once, as a gestalt, as in the saying, *A picture is worth a thousand words*. The experience of listening to and being with a patient in session feels much the same. We take in meaning not just from the patient's words but from their bodily nonverbals, which add layers of understanding that remain implicit until we find a way to make them explicit.

When writing an essay or a symphony, setting up a scientific study, or bringing forth anything new, the right hemisphere creates the raw first narrative—the sloppy copy—which has a beginning, middle, and end. The right sends that rough draft to the left for revision and polishing. The left's contribution may spark a new idea from the right hemisphere, which then needs further modification from the left, which may spark another idea from the right, and so on. When this dance, called *flow*, is going well—when the right hemisphere is in charge—it is associated with a profound sense of well-being and aliveness (Csikszentmihalyi, 2008). We are immersed and don't notice time passing, for that requires self-consciousness (a left-brain function), which disappears when in a flow state (when right brain leads).

Let's return now to the sloppy first draft I shared above. A week or so after I wrote it, I reread it. Bestselling author Stephen King (2000) recommends taking a break between first drafts and revision.

> How long you let your book rest—sort of like bread dough between kneadings—is entirely up to you. . . . When you come to the correct evening (which you well may have marked on your office calendar) take your manuscript out of the drawer. If it looks like an alien relic bought at a junk-shop or yard sale where you can hardly remember stopping, you're ready. (p. 211)

The idea here is that enough time has passed that you can read your draft as if you hadn't written it—

objectively and with an open mind. In other words, with right-brain acceptance, instead of left-brain rejection. My left hemisphere immediately corrected all the grammatical errors and deleted what was obviously unnecessary. But then my right hemisphere had an idea or two. I added a few lines, which the left tweaked, and after a few back-and-forths, the following is their joint product:

Your husband swings your 14-month old into your hands. You gather her in your arms, kiss the top of her downy head, and inhale her sweet baby smell. He gives you both a kiss and heads off to work. You're too hopped up from your graveyard shift at the hospital to sleep, so you strap Mandy into her car seat and drive to Donalli Brothers Meats to see Uncle Vinny. The sun is bright this late spring morning. When you walk into the commercial kitchen, you are blind for a minute. The metallic smell of raw meat enfolds you. Mandy sits on your hip held in one arm, her rolling walker in the other hand. Doors bang and clank, boxes thump and slither, water runs from a tap somewhere deeper in.

"Carol!" a gravelly voice calls from across the room. Mandy reaches out her arms, cooing.

"Hi Uncle Vinny!" You walk toward his voice and he materializes from the gloom, a tall man in a blood-splattered white apron. "I'm getting ready to grind burger," he says, pointing to a massive pile of red chuck sitting on the metal table in front of him. "Put the baby here, beside the grinder, so she can watch." You set up her walker and stand Mandy in it. She holds the rim with both hands. He tosses brick sized chunks of meat into the funnel of the grinder. Pink curly strings pour from the grinder into the ginormous bowl. Mandy laughs. Vinny makes googly-eyed faces at her, "Hey, little girl, watch this!" and juggles pieces of meat in the air. She crows with delight, mouth open, eyes full of wonder.

The first draft was 379 words, the revision 280 despite the presence of new details. With redundancies and irrelevancies eliminated, the arc of the first draft stands, yet it's a livelier and leaner read. (I'll spare you my left hemisphere's commentary.) Suffice it to say the two hemispheres produce better work together than either does alone.

However, as we've learned, the two hemispheres often don't work well together. Artists who regularly birth new work know newborn drafts should not be evaluated and critiqued immediately after delivery. Instead, as Stephen King suggests, it's best to wait a few days, or weeks. Without that delay, feedback from the verbal left hemisphere will be negative—it rejects what it doesn't recognize—and because its voice is loud and verbal, we hear it in our heads, consciously. It speaks authoritatively, as if it's an expert on creating, but how can it be? The left knows nothing about creating. The qualities that make the left excellent at revising and polishing are also what make it critical, bossy, self-conscious, and resistant to change. It's a loud and nasty know-it-all, aka The Critic. Yielding to it in the immediate aftermath of creating a first draft results in derivative work.

The following strategies help curb the, but can't fully eliminate, left hemisphere's doom-and-glooming when engaged in a creative project:

1. The timer forces the right hemisphere to bring that first, rough draft to a close.
2. Deferring reviewing that first effort for a while inhibits the left's automatic rejection of new material.
3. Once the material becomes familiar through review and the revision process is well along, perfectionism becomes another danger. The left

hemisphere gets easily caught in in its own dissatisfaction loop and resists transferring the material back to the right. Again, a deadline helps—it has the power to break that gridlock with external pressure. The book, cartoon, or grant proposal will never be perfect, but it *must be submitted* by a specific date regardless. Otherwise, the book or cartoon won't be published or the grant money awarded.

4. Accept that this state of tension *is* the creative process.

Tell the truth through whichever veil comes to hand—but tell it. Resign yourself to the lifelong sadness that comes from never being satisfied.

— ZADIE SMITH, *White Teeth*

Right-Brain Patients, Left-Brain Therapists

The right hemisphere knows without knowing, that is to say, without verbal consciousness. It thinks in images. "What is an image? The formless thing which gives things form" (Barry, 2008, p. 8). The right understands the implicit, as well as the primacy of bodily experience that expresses itself in the language of metaphor.

> *Metaphor* is not just a reflection of what has been . . . but the *means whereby the truly new,* rather than just the novel, *may come about.* [emphasis mine] When a metaphor actually lives in the mind it can generate new thoughts or understanding—it is cognitively real and active, not just a dead historical remnant of a once live metaphor, a cliché. All understanding, whether of the world or even of ourselves, depends on choosing the right metaphor. The metaphor we choose governs what we see. (McGilchrist, 2009, p. 179)

When we usher a patient into our office, that starts the timer on the narrative arc of the session, which by its end will tell a story. But the session is also part of a larger, ongoing narrative, which can be thought of as a way of understanding a series of events that reflects and promotes a particular point of view or set of values (Cohen-Sheehy et al., 2021). When patient and therapist bring their individual attentions and personal narratives to bear on the treatment, that brings the treatment *relationship* into being as a third entity.

Let's consider the following metaphor. What if the patient functions in session and in the overall treatment as the right hemisphere, and the clinician as the left?

That allows us to understand the treatment relationship as a creative work in process, one that is cocreated by patient and clinician, session by session, in much the same way that a novelist's right and left hemispheres work together to write the chapters that ultimately become a novel.

The patient, as right hemisphere, delivers to the therapist undifferentiated raw material—the rough draft or sloppy copy. The therapist, as left hemisphere, "listens" closely—this includes taking in other nonverbal communications—to what the patient reveals. The therapist also maintains the "frame" of the session by honoring its deadline, ending as scheduled. Over time, the session's duration becomes a routine the patient takes for granted, ultimately surrendering its control to us. The session acquires a sense of timelessness, which facilitates the release of free associations and transference reactions: right-hemisphere raw material. "The experience has much in common with that of the dream, and the analyst's announcement that 'time is up' might be compared with an alarm clock that awakens the patient from a dreamlike experience" (Hartocollis, 2003, p. 951).

Throughout the session, and out of consciousness, the patient's right hemisphere tracks the time remaining while his left hemisphere simultaneously judges, criticizes, and inhibits what he reveals to the therapist. We tend to assume that what holds back patients from telling us painful information earlier in the session (rather than at the last minute) is that they need more time in treatment to trust us. That presumes building trust is based on duration of treatment: the longer the treatment, the more trust. But I've had well-established patients in decades-long treatments drop doorknob bombshells, which calls that premise into question.

Of course, trust matters—it is the bedrock of the treatment relationship. In fact, the trust between patient and therapist supports the patient's right hemisphere's desire to share something new and sensitive, though doing so will leave them vulnerable to the therapist's judgment. Meanwhile, the patient's risk-averse left hemisphere inhibits the impulse in order to maintain the status quo.

The psychoanalytic literature (Gabbard, Gans, Brody, Arnd-Caddigan, among others; see Chapter 1) presumes this internal tug-of-war is based on the patient's past, transference to the therapist, and less commonly, therapist countertransference. In other words, a last-minute disclosure, occurring within the standardized psychoanalytic time frame of forty-five minutes, is driven by interpersonal and intrapsychic material specific to the patient and therapist. Knowing that the therapist will be closing the session imminently, the last-minute exit line or doorknob moment is the patient's compromise between "saying it and not saying it" (Gabbard, 1980, p. 580). The material is so emotionally charged, the patient can only express it on her way out the door and then bolt, so as to avoid discussion.

But non-mental health professionals I know report that their clients—surprise—drop doorknob moments at the end of appointments with them, too, as they do among physicians (see Chapter 1). The appointments vary in length, but as with therapists, trust is the foundation of the client's relationship with these different professionals, be they lawyers, brokers, financial planners, or healthcare providers.

"Yeah. Doorknob moments," my dentist said, as he drilled off a temporary crown and then tapped on the permanent one. "Let me tell you about a doozy. I had worked for hours on this client, applying new crowns and replacing old ones on most of his molars—his mouth was a mess. Finally, we're done. He turns to me with his hand on the doorknob and says, 'Doc, I gotta tell you. I lost all my money at the casino last night.' "

If his hands hadn't been in my open mouth already, my jaw would have dropped. The first chance I got, I asked, "What did you do?!"

"Put him on a payment plan. And changed my payment policy for crowns. Payment up front."

As another example, my husband and I are in private practice, which is a small business. When there are issues with software, payroll, taxes, and anything else outside my wheelhouse, I consult with Leslie, who provides "financial managerial analysis" for small businesses.

Leslie arrived late for our last lunch meeting—she is often late—because when she told her previous client she had to go, he said, "Just one more thing."

"I'd just spent two hours with him!" she said.

"What did you do?"

"I stayed," she said, exasperated with herself. "When I got up to leave after another half hour, he said just-one-more-thing again!"

"And . . . ?"

"I was already late to meet you. I left."

"Well, unlike with us therapists, I guess business doorknob moments aren't ever life or death, right?"

"No. But clients *always* think their business is life or death."

I flashed back to the residency and the attending who'd said, *Remember, the patient's emergency is not necessarily your emergency. You need to make that determination for yourself and proceed accordingly.*

"How often do you agree with the client that his doorknob moment needs to be addressed right away?" I asked Leslie.

"Sometimes. But mostly it can wait. They just don't want to."

"So . . . , you usually run over?"

"Yeah." She paused. "Why is it so hard for clients— he's not the only one—to let me go? It's like they get desperate they'll never see me again!"

"That's interesting. What would they be desperate about?"

"I don't know! But it's hard to say no."

"You know . . . ," I said, raising my eyebrows and leaning in with comical irony, "I can help you with *that*."

She laughed.

"Seriously, have you tried telling them up front you have to leave at say, 2:30. And it's a hard 2:30 because you have another appointment?"

"Yeah, I know I should do that more. But some clients wouldn't honor it. Others would say, 'It's 2:30, don't you need to go?'" She laughed at herself.

"How often does it happen that a client says just-one-more-thing when time is up?"

"Every day!"

Certainly, non-mental health professionals and their clients experience transference and countertransference reactions. How could they not? But that frame of reference is so distant from their area of expertise, it might as well be in outer space.

That doorknob moments happen in a variety of professions, not just mental health, suggests that the phenomenon is independent of content, as well as appointment length. If that's so, then the *structural element*—the impending deadline or *end of the session*—may play a part in making the disclosure happen: no deadline, no revelation. As discussed above, artists know this and use it when producing new work.

What if, in any timed consultation of any length, the client, like the patient, functions as the right hemisphere, and the professional, like the therapist, as the left? If so, then it is the client's/patient's job as right hemisphere to close the narrative arc of the appointment, one option of many being the doorknob moment, or cliffhanger.

What if, as the earlier, informal review of creative processes suggests, the right hemisphere *needs* a time constraint to finish and deliver new work to the public? What if it is the physical deadline (timer, submission date, end of meeting) that enables the right hemisphere to break the gridlock caused by the left's opposition? Could it be that it is the appointment's imminent end— the deadline—that actually *causes* the patient/client to deliver a doorknob moment? As in, she *wouldn't have released it otherwise?*

The specifics of the revelation, whether transference issues to a therapist, medical concerns to a primary care doctor, or financial concerns to financial planner, add meaning and history without invalidating the structural motivator provided by the impending end of the session. When a patient/client has reached the tipping point of disclosure—surely determined by multiple variables—maybe it's simply a matter of the deadline providing that final gentle shove. To requote Ann Patchett (2003), "When I can't think of another stall, when putting it off has actually become more painful than doing it . . . " (p. 25) that's when she starts actually writing.

What if emotionally charged disclosures in any setting happen at the last minute simply because that's the way the brain works? This construct is ahistorical and does not address what the disclosure means in the context of the treatment. However, it suggests that doorknob moments are inescapable because they reliably occur in relationship to this structural element of the frame: the impending end, or deadline. Trusting the session will end on time, the patient's right hemisphere decides the risk of disclosing new material is worth taking.

Meanwhile, clinicians functioning as left hemisphere need the session to end on time too. Because our left hemispheres reject what is new, unfamiliar, and unsettling, we are at risk, in running over time, to react in a way that doesn't help the patient or the treatment. Between sessions, our left hemisphere finds the familiar in what the patient has shared, processes it, and sends it to our right hemisphere, which reframes and incorporates it into the unfolding narrative of the treatment to date. When to share these gleaned insights is a clinical judgment call. Our right hemispheres' creativity and ability to problem solve the current state of play are empowered by holding the deadline because it reins in the understandable and caring, but *not necessarily helpful*, impulse to run over time in the face of patient distress.

Has any research been done to support this idea? I couldn't find any. While we wait for the neuropsychiatric evidence to emerge, I've found considering doorknob bombshells within this organizing principle clinically grounding. Excluding a medical emergency, even if the patient is sobbing heartbrokenly, this formulation decreases my worry that closing the session as scheduled will cause her more suffering. Or, put the other way, my confidence increases that closing on time is the therapeutic thing to do (although as Arnd-Caddigan [2013] suggests, if the patient desires it, and you have the time, deem it therapeutic, and are willing to process fallout with the next scheduled patient who is kept waiting, prolonging the session remains an option).

In subsequent sessions, either or both parties may share insights precipitated by the doorknob moment. Thus, the last-minute disclosure serves both as the end of the current session and as the beginning of the next installment in the larger creative work in progress (Gabbard, 1982; Gans, 2016). Individual session arcs link together to form the ongoing metanarrative that is treatment similar to the way chapters link plots and subplots in a novel. Thus, narrative structure also contains the accumulated insights and information of multiple earlier sessions.

Seasoned clinician Louis Cozolino (2021) observes that as we become more skillful and get more deeply into the work, understanding treatment as an evolving story allows us to shift away from the need for information and control, toward becoming more comfortable with uncertainty, exploration, and wisdom.

The Role of Chance in Creative Processes and in Sessions

Twyla Tharp notes that habitually creative people are, in E. B. White's phrase, "prepared to be lucky." The key words, she says, are prepared and lucky. "They are inseparable." In creative endeavors, the right and left hemispheres work together more often than they are at odds.

> You don't get lucky without preparation, and there's no sense in being prepared if you're not open to the

possibility of a glorious accident. . . . Some people resent the idea of luck. Accepting the role of chance in our lives suggests that our creations and triumphs are not entirely our own, and that in some way we're undeserving of our success. I say, Get over it. This is how the world works. *In creative endeavors luck is a skill* [emphasis mine]. (Tharp, 2003, p. 120)

Luck is a skill. This statement is ambiguous and par-adoxical in the way of Heraclitus's: No one ever steps in the same river twice. We usually think of luck as an outside force, separate from ourselves, something that happens randomly *to* us. And that's true. But it's also true that the more deeply we practice our craft, the more alert we become to unforeseen circumstance, and the more creatively we are able to use it to move the treatment forward. That's the sense in which luck and skill become one.

Managing luck is the domain of the right hemi-sphere; acquiring skill, the left's. When they work well together, the right is in charge. However, when our left hemisphere hijacks control of our mind, we can lose our ability to see the treatment in context, and our ability to clinically use the unexpected diminishes. When the left hemisphere is impaired by, for example, a stroke, creativity can also be enhanced. Conversely, splitting the corpus callosum impairs creativity. That's because the corpus callosum's primary function is to both separate and connect the two hemispheres. Creativity depends on the union of things that are usually kept separated (McGilchrist, 2009).

The creative process requires both hemispheres, as does therapy. If you have been a practicing therapist for a while, you'll immediately recognize that how we manage unexpected interactions is a crucial aspect of our work. No matter how skillful we are, there is no avoiding the unexpected in session. Coping therapeutically with these moments requires a tolerance for uncertainty, for mistakes, and for awkwardness, all of which are managed by the right-brain.

Regardless, our left hemispheres will insist we should have anticipated the unexpected and should have handled it with aplomb. This is a lie and a crutch that allows us to assume we can, in fact, have everything under control—which, being human, is an impossible expectation to meet. It's a mindfulness practice to ignore the left's faultfinding. If you are a perfectionist, push back by giving yourself permission to make mistakes. It's okay. Our function in the treatment relationship is to help the patient, not to be perfect.

Additionally, it's important to avoid going with the first idea that comes to mind as a response to what the patient offers. This is another reason why it is helpful (for us) to end on time in the face of a doorknob moment. Doing so allows us to mull things over between sessions, instead of reacting reflexively in the moment. We need time to remain open to other ideas that might follow and prove productive to the treatment's forward motion. It's an "unshakable rule that you don't have a really good idea until you combine two little ideas" (Tharp, 2003, p. 97).

The right hemisphere churns out ideas without heed for quality or need to choose. Meanwhile, the left demands certainty and closure. Thus, anxiety and uncertainty are always present, in greater or lesser degree, when we engage creatively with a project or a patient. Rather than interpret this as a problem, it is more fruitful to "expect the unexpected" (Barry, 1999) in session and to recognize it for what it is: an opportunity.

> To embrace luck, you have to enhance your tolerance for ambiguity. Plan only to a point. The great military strategists from Sun-Tzu to Clausewitz have advised that you can plan only so far into the

battle; you have to save lots of room for your adver-
sary's contribution. (Tharp, 2003, p. 123)

Ditto in therapy. We need to leave lots of room for the
patient to contribute something new, be it a random
aha of insight during session or a last-minute revelation.

Modeling Patience for Our Patients

The kind of attention we pay actually alters the
world; we are literally partners in creation.

— IAIN MCGILCHRIST, *The Master and His Emissary:
The Divided Brain and the Making of the Western World*

While we are trained to avoid disclosing personal
information in session (that takes the patient's attention off them and puts it onto us, a distraction from
the work), much as we try, it is impossible to withhold
everything of ourselves from astute patients who can
read body language as well as we can. Nor should we
want to. *Luck is a skill.* If we're not defensive about
what patients notice about us, how we handle that
moment of personal exposure can make a constructive
difference to the treatment, as happened in this example from my practice.

My patient Dave's adult daughter Janet caused him heartache for she'd married a man who was wrong for her, with predictable and dismaying consequences. "I love her so much!" Dave said. "All I want is to protect her from getting hurt."

"Yes, that's the rub with adult children," I said, thinking of my own son, then twenty-one. "If they don't ask our opinion, we have no authority to intervene. We can try anyway. But if they still don't listen, we're forced to watch, like rubbernecking an impending crash."

My ability to predict what the consequences of certain choices might be is often helpful to patients. They grant me the authority to provide feedback on their interpersonal dilemmas, so they can understand themselves better, which then opens up different and new options in future when they find themselves in a similar situation. But parenting carries a deeper emotional investment because of the love attachment. The empathic suffering from watching a beloved child make disastrous choices is particularly acute. I flashed back to what I'd gone through with my son when he was eighteen. He had started his first year at the local college, kept his part-time job at Game Stop, and moved into the studio above our office.

Initially he came over to the house a lot, but as fall rolled into winter, and winter into spring, he called and came over less and less. He always had a reason—he had to study for a test, he had plans, he had to work, he was tired. When our favorite soft-serve ice cream shop opened after Memorial Day, I stopped into Game Stop to see if he wanted to go after his shift. The kid behind the counter told me he hadn't worked there since February. I was dumb-struck. *He'd been lying! Why?!*

His father and I insisted he come over for dinner that night, and it all came out. He wasn't seeing his friends and hadn't for months. He quit the job rather than not show up. He was barely getting to class and spent most days in bed. He'd lied that he was fine. He'd lied that he was working. "I don't know why I lied," he said. "But the longer I didn't tell you, the more I couldn't tell you." He'd suffered a vegetative depression alone for two semesters, not uncommon in kids his age. His father and I are psychiatrists. We could have helped him!

As Dave told me how his daughter Janet shut him out, I acknowledged the suffering that goes with the resulting helplessness. "I don't think any parent of adult kids escapes. I certainly haven't with my son."

We took a moment of silence to be with that ghastly reality. He looked in my eyes with compassion and said, "I can see how deeply sad that makes you."

I caught my breath, pierced to the core. He had bypassed all my defenses speaking this truth, which until that moment I had avoided. For three years, I had stayed on the surface, focusing on my frustration and worry. But sadness was the only possible response to how little, if any, control I had over how my son chose to live *his* life. My love couldn't protect him, especially if he shut me out.

I got it. And it hurt. I closed my eyes. When I opened them, I looked at Dave with the wonder and astonishment that comes with an aha moment. I was also uncomfortably aware that I felt emotionally naked before him. I took a big breath. "Wow," I said. "You're right. Thank you."

He smiled and nodded. There was a long silence while I processed this radical, new place I was in with him. I didn't want to deny that he'd affected me profoundly. After all, he'd just given me a huge gift. But I also needed to return to my professional self. How to affirm him while regaining my composure? I chose humor. I smiled, "Send me your bill."

He burst out laughing and I joined him. The atmosphere in the room became fresh and green as it does after a cleansing rain. His attention had literally changed me, which changed him. With that, the treatment relationship changed too. Our right hemispheres, in charge of empathic connection, made that possible.

While my aha moment with Dave was positively transformative, being even fleetingly stripped of one's defenses isn't pleasant. Growth can be painful. Most of the time, the gain is worth the pain. Sometimes, though, an aha is too much, as happened with another patient.

Natalie was forty, married with two young children, in tenuous recovery for a few years from twenty years of alcohol abuse, and in treatment for depression. Our work together made her aware that she engaged with many other activities, such as online shopping and gaming, in the same way she had previously used alcohol. So, when I observed she was behaving similarly having a tempestuous affair, I didn't expect her to react the way she did. She suffered a crushing aha moment, one that stopped her cold.

"What?!" she'd cried with deep dismay. "This is who I am? I do this *everywhere*? With *everything*? *All the time*? Fuck!" She slumped back in the upholstered chair, radiating disgust and hopelessness.

Unfortunately, shortly thereafter, the pandemic shutdown happened and we were forced to switch to phone work. Several productive months later, she ended the affair. But her dysphoria persisted.

"A core aspect of the mind can be defined as an embodied and relational process that regulates the flow of energy and information" (Siegel, 2012, p. xxvi). My comment linking the affair to her drinking behavior apparently triggered an aha in Natalie that disrupted her ability to regulate her internal flow of energy and information—she couldn't find her "sea legs" in that new environment. Unlike with my patient Phillip (of the Midnight Page), referencing her aha moment in future sessions didn't help her. Within the year, her husband discovered she'd been having phone sex with his best friend, and she lost what she valued most: her marriage, family life, and social standing.

What we each, patient and therapist, choose to reveal and put our attention on in session carries consequences. That's true for what we don't attend to as well;

the consequence will simply be different. Earlier in my career, I would have blamed myself for Natalie's reaction and agonized over what I'd missed, could have done differently, and so on. But that would make her response all about me, which is unacceptably egocentric.

In addiction, the left hemisphere with its me-first attitude hijacks control of the mind–brain (McGilchrist, 2009). Perhaps, despite her technical sobriety, Natalie's left hemisphere was still in charge and driving her self-defeating behavior without regard for context and consequences. Perhaps my observation broke through that denial. Or maybe I misread her ability to receive it. Or possibly we both contributed. What part the pandemic and remote work played remains unclear. It's an uncomfortable truth that aha moments occur unpredictably and have unpredictable consequences.

Being two separate individuals, therapist and patient will likely find specific sessions meaningful and memorable in different ways (Yalom & Elkin, 1991). However, what we discuss together in session as part of the ongoing narrative of treatment, with its themes and variations, does allow us to occasionally agree on a specific incident as emblematic and representative of a particular psychodynamic theme, as Phillip and I did with the Midnight Page.

Narratives bridge the divide between distant events in episodic memory. We retain both events and story lines from the treatment in episodic memory, a type of long-term memory that involves conscious recollection of previous experiences with their context in terms of time, place, and associated emotions (Cohen-Sheehy et al., 2021). This allows either of us to reference an iconic incident when a variation on its theme comes up. That can move the treatment forward, as with Phillip and the Midnight Page, but not always, as with Natalie.

It's heartbreaking how often what we say to a patient, no matter how carefully thought through and worded, fails to transmit. Words are so often inadequate, and so easily misinterpreted. Ann Patchett (2013) offers a way to live with this constant reminder of our limitations:

> I believe, more than anything, that *this grief of constantly having to face down our own inadequacies* [emphasis mine] is what keeps people from being writers [And in therapy work, what burns us out]. *Forgiveness, therefore, is key* [emphasis mine]. I can't write the book I want to write, but I can and will write the book I am capable of writing. Again and again throughout the course of my life I will forgive myself. (pp. 29–30)

So too, I remind myself: I can't be the therapist I want to be, but I can and will be the therapist I am capable of being. Again and again throughout my working life I will forgive myself. I remind myself also of Horney's (1950) admonition about the limits of what we can accomplish:

> We must be clear about the seriousness of the involvement [of intrapsychic defenses] in order to guard against false optimism, envisioning quick and easy cures. . . . We cannot "cure" the wrong course which the development of a person has taken. We can only assist him in gradually outgrowing his difficulties so that his development may assume a more constructive course. (p. 333)

We are models for our patients. The more patience we have for ourselves, the more we will have for them, and the more they may come, in time, to have for themselves. Even as we have trouble forgiving ourselves our errors and limitations, imagine what patients go through flattening terrifying, three-dimensional, visceral, and sensory experience into two-dimensional words, *in the hope we'll understand.* The vulnerability and leap of faith the therapy process requires of patients are breath-taking. After all, we are strangers— compassionate strangers, but still strangers. In kind, we clinicians must have the equivalent faith in ourselves—that we are able to receive what we are given and then go on to actually be helpful, despite our human limitations.

CHAPTER 5

The Surprisingly Useful Consequences of Honoring the Session Deadline

This chapter combines the ideas described in the previous chapters to argue that consistently ending on time builds trust, helps prevent treatment stagnation, and shifts the locus of control from outside forces to inside resources—for both clinician and patient.

Axioms

So, let's go with the right-brain patients/left-brain clinicians metaphor. Let's also assume therapy is a creative work in progress with patient and therapist cocreating the treatment, session by session, just as a novelist uses both right and left hemispheres to write a novel, chapter by chapter. Finally, let's agree that holding the deadline—ending the session on time—catalyzes patients to release new information.

Functioning as right hemisphere, patients deliver new material to the treatment within the time frame, or narrative arc, of the session. They are responsible for closing the arc, with one option being the cliff-hanger, or doorknob bombshell. Therapists, functioning as left hemisphere, are responsible for holding the session deadline—ending on time. Between sessions we take time to focus on, clarify, and make explicit what we recognize within the complexity and ambiguity of patients' revelations.

While it can be risky and anxiety provoking for the patient—her right hemisphere must overcome the naysaying of her left—disclosure of new information is necessary to prevent treatment stagnation. This may seem obvious, but making it safe for patients to disclose what they are afraid to reveal is hardly straightforward. Without their generosity, we would have nothing to work with.

To requote Yalom (2002), the paramount task of therapist and patient "is to build a relationship together that will itself become the agent of change" (p. 34). For the treatment relationship to have that power, trust between patient and therapist is essential. The nature of patients' attachment to us and their level of trust depends on how secure/insecure they feel with us and, by extension, with others. We facilitate patients' level of trust and security by behaving consistently and reliably in the treatment relationship. Predictably ending the session on time is one way.

Security broadly refers to that internal, *felt* sense of being able to rely on another person and that a healthy form of interdependence is not only possible but exists. The sense of self is open, and interactions with others are rewarding. Developmentally, sensitive caregiving from a parent is thought to create this mental model of security in a child, which allows the child to explore the world, feel good about herself, and find close, satisfying connections with others (Siegel, 2012).

Conversely, insensitive caregiving gives rise to (broadly) one of three types of insecurity in a child, which carries forward into adulthood, and our offices. The first, *ambivalent* or *resistant attachment*, arises when caregivers or parents are inconsistent and intrusive. The child learns that she cannot rely on that attachment figure to soothe and protect her, which makes her chronically anxious. In adulthood, ambivalently attached people maximize their attachment system— their social network—by being excessively clingy and needy of reassurance. Intimate partners end up feeling helpless—their anxious partner is a "bottomless pit of neediness" with "nothing being quite good enough" (Siegel, 2012, pp. 21–23).

The second, *avoidance attachment*, results when the child is not seen and not reliably attuned to by the primary caregiver. The child adapts by avoiding needing that particular caregiver and that particular relationship. Thankfully, that doesn't prevent a child from having a secure, or ambivalent, attachment with another caregiver. "Studies reveal that even with . . . avoidance as a survival strategy, the child still 'knows' . . . that relationships do matter. Adults with this stance also show implicit, inward, neural signs of needing others" (Siegel, 2012, pp. 21–23). Adults with this learned strategy avoid or minimize expressing a need for others in their outward actions. Their romantic partners often feel rejected, unneeded, and isolated from their loved one.

A third form of insecurity, *disorganized attachment*, can arise when there is both excessive approach (arousing intense fear) and excessive avoidance (causing withdrawal). Here the caregiver is both a source of terror and the child's source of protection. Two mutually opposed neurological systems kick in: one tells the child to flee from this dangerous person, while the other tells her to go toward that same person for protection. The child is caught in an inescapable neurological double bind. Her internal world breaks down, fragmenting her sense of self, which may result in pathological dissociation. This combination of approach and withdrawal is neurologically traumatic and leads to a disorganized form of insecure attachment, one that has the most negative outcomes in adulthood (Siegel, 2012).

The psychotherapy approaches I've discussed throughout this book require interpersonal trust in the here-and-now therapy relationship to help the patient outgrow dysfunctional behaviors originating in the past. Unfortunately, these have not been particularly helpful for patients suffering from trauma-shattered trust. Interestingly, Bessel van der Kolk (2014), a leader in research and treatment of PTSD, suggests that a non-relational intervention, eye movement desensitization and reprocessing (EMDR), may prove helpful to these patients. How EMDR works isn't clear, but three things seem to be the case. First, EMDR affects the mind/brain in some way that gives people rapid access to loosely associated memories and images from their past. This appears to help them put the traumatic experience(s) into a larger context or perspective. Second, people may be able to heal from trauma *without talking about it*. EMDR enables them to observe their experiences in a new way, without verbal give and take with another person. Lastly, EMDR can help even if patient and therapist *do not have a trusting relationship.* This is

> particularly intriguing because trauma, understandably, rarely leaves people with an open, trusting heart. . . . Because EMDR doesn't require patients to speak about the intolerable or explain to a therapist why they feel so upset, it allows them to stay fully focused on their internal experience with sometimes extraordinary results. (p. 255)

Anxiously and avoidantly insecure patients, possibly even disorganizedly insecure patients, may present new material at any point in the session. But in my experience, the more sensitive and highly guarded the material is, the more likely they are to release it at the last possible minute as a doorknob bombshell, or exit line (Gabbard, 1982). The impending end of the session—the structural deadline—somehow empowers patients' right hemisphere to take the risk of disclosing painful information to their therapist, overriding their left hemisphere's objections.

This is not without danger for a patient. Once the revelation is out in public, it can never be private again. Revealing the raw self always leaves patients exposed and vulnerable to our judgment. They often break down, and their distress can be heartbreaking for us to bear. It can be exceedingly difficult to overcome the understandable and caring impulse to intervene. This is the moment—a matter of seconds—when we have to decide whether to end as scheduled or run over.

An Argument for Not Prolonging the Session

To keep revealing new material, patients need to trust us. Going with the hypothesis that patients release sensitive information *because* they are counting on us to hold the deadline and end as scheduled, running over time sends patients two undesirable, nonverbal messages:

1. We are unpredictable, therefore untrustworthy.
2. *We* don't trust *them* to rally without us.

With the first message, we violate the do-no-harm rule—lack of predictability arouses anxiety and distrust. With the second, we potentially collude with and/

or foster unhealthy codependence and, again, violate the do-no-harm rule.

The concept of codependence emerged from the substance abuse literature to describe the dysfunctional relationship dynamic that results when one person in the dyad, the alcoholic/addict, "takes" too much, and the other, the enabler, "gives" too much. The meaning of "codependence" has generalized into common vernacular to describe any relationship in which one person is overfunctioning as a caregiver without reciprocity from the other. The term is controversial because it implies that being nurturing, supportive, and loving of an impaired loved one is part of the problem. This ignores the reality that we are hard-wired to take care of our loved one(s), especially when they are ill, in trouble, or unable in other ways to take care of themselves.

"Coregulation" is a more specific, science-based term for the continuous, dynamic process of information exchange, both verbal and nonverbal, between two people in a relationship.

Science reveals clearly that our social world directly shapes how our neural firing unfolds. The studies illuminate how we help one another regulate our internal states through attuning to the internal states of the other person as part of what is called mutual regulation, co-regulation, or dyadic regulation. . . . From an interpersonal neurobiology perspective of the mind as an embodied and embedded process, we can understand how relationship connections and neural connections both contribute fully to the creation of our physiological equilibrium and our mental reality. (Siegel, 2012, § 15, p. 3)

How does this apply to ending the session as scheduled, in the wake of a patient becoming distraught following a last-minute revelation? Let's be honest with ourselves: being caring, functional, and helpful—by temperament and training—we are vulnerable in that moment to prolong the session simply out of a desire to help. Such an intervention is essentially impulsive and done without deliberation. Our left hemisphere—just like our patient's, just like everyone's—doesn't like being faced with something new at any time, much less having to cope quickly. What we say or don't say, do or don't do under the pressure of that moment might later prove to have been unhelpful to the patient.

Artists who regularly create new work know that first drafts shouldn't be reviewed, judged, and criticized immediately afterward (Kent & Steward, 2008). Feedback from the verbal self (left hemisphere) is almost always negative because it rejects what is new in favor of what is familiar. "Don't try to create and analyze at the same time. They are different processes" (a quote by Corita Kent, popularized in the 1960s by John Cage). Attempting to do both simultaneously results in "analysis paralysis" or, to paraphrase Ann Patchett (2013), editing yourself off the page.

I have found that a similar sort of mental paralysis happens to me if I find myself running over attempting to process a patient's disclosure reactively, that is, without deliberation. Patients will stay as long as I let them, and they cling when I attempt to close. A covert power struggle ensues between us, mirroring the conflict occurring between my left and right hemispheres (metaphorically, of course, not biologically). With each minute that passes, it becomes more difficult to decide what to do, which increases the risk that I will be clumsy and say something unfortunate in attempting to close the session.

That's what happened with my patient Joe, who up to the following moment had been coming in for twenty-minute medication management sessions for treatment of obsessive-compulsive disorder.

Just as I said, "We need to wrap up," he said, "One more thing Doc. My wife left me last week and took our daughter with her." Ordinarily stoic, he teared up, looked down, and clasped his hands tightly in his lap.

"What?!" I responded without thinking. With that, he was off, a torrent of words gushing forth. I felt unbearably sorry for him and also unbearably trapped. I listened for an opening, frozen between wanting to helpfully intervene, which wasn't realistic given we were out of time, and needing to close. Fifteen minutes of the next patient's session flew by during which Joe never paused for breath.

Finally, I forced myself to cut him off: "Joe! We need to stop!" He came to, surfacing reluctantly from his troubles. I relaxed my voice to a more soothing timbre: "How about you come in next week for a full session?" Since it was too late to be tactful, I immediately stood up to cue him he needed to go.

"I just have to tell you one more thing," he said desperately.

I shook my head, "I'm sorry, we've run out of time. Let's start with that at our next session."

He glowered but trailed behind me to my office manager's desk, where she'd give him an appoint-

ment. "See you next week," I said over my shoulder,
heading straight for the waiting room.

Bottom line: *we, too, need the session to end on time*,
to prevent ourselves from sharing impulsive, un-
thought-through reactions with potentially negative
consequences. Joe took my spontaneous response to his
last-minute news as permission to tell me more, which
overwhelmed me. I was unable to simultaneously process what was happening and problem-solve it, much
less send him on his way gracefully. The time to mull
over and identify what can be used from new material
the patient gives us at the last minute is *after* the session ends, and before the next one. Insights gleaned can
then be shared strategically in future sessions to move
the treatment forward.

Most important, not ending on time is a structural
inconsistency, which if repeated over time has the
potential to undermine patients' trust. The patient's
right hemisphere notes this breach of reliability (out of
consciousness) and may stop delivering cliff-hangers. If
a treatment is stagnating, this may be why.

I've been reassured to find that most patients, even
when sobbing piteously, leave willingly and quickly if I
hold the line and say we must end now. Why? Because

they have done their job: time to go. Patients need the bulk of the session to work up to delivering the revelation (again, whether knowingly or unknowingly). They may not need or want my immediate response, for various reasons, the most straightforward of which is mental fatigue. Overcoming resistance is exhausting. Being emotionally exhausted just adds another layer to their vulnerability to us, should we prolong the session instead of closing.

Before this formulation came to me, the patient's level of distress following a last-minute disclosure influenced when I ended the session—the locus of control was outside me. Now, I (mostly) end the session on time because I am confident it *is* the therapeutic thing to do—the locus of control is inside me. Even better, the patient experiences the same empowerment.

I now prepare patients for the inevitability of a doorknob revelation when introducing them to the ground rules about the therapy/treatment process— confidentiality, the need for full disclosure, how to receive here-and-now feedback, and so forth. I predict that they will, eventually, find themselves upset by something they've revealed at session's end. I educate them that this is how the brain delivers new and sensitive information but we'll have to end on time regardless, *because they wouldn't have told me otherwise.*

Patients are reassured to be reminded in the wake of a doorknob moment that this is part of the therapy process. Their locus of control shifts from outside—something random is happening *to* them—to inside: it's happened *because* of them. Though we must end on time now, I say, we'll discuss this at the next session, or if you'd like, in an extra session.

This formulation eliminates the need for us to make a judgment call under time pressure. Even better, it empowers us to end on time by blocking the natural impulse to intervene and prolong the session when a patient becomes distraught following a last-minute disclosure. I can tolerate a great deal of patient upset if I am confident that ending on time guarantees a safe therapeutic environment, facilitates trust, and enables the patient to release new material, which keeps the treatment lively. Ending the session skillfully in the face of patient upset becomes a different but much more manageable challenge. Admittedly, it is often hard to do. Practice makes better.

A Few Variations on the Doorknob Moment

Since we should expect and, indeed, welcome doorknob bombshells, here are several variations I've experienced over the years with my patients, along with some strategies that have worked for me. There is the medical emergency and the false emergency, the personal attack and the flatterer, as well as my own occasional blunder and, sometimes, the patient who puts me on the spot.

The Caveat

My patient Kate, while putting on her coat to leave, tells me she'd taken a month's worth of lithium two hours before the session, after a fight with her boyfriend. It goes without saying, but I'll say it anyway: a medical emergency requires crisis intervention, which voids all other considerations. A lithium overdose can kill you. I call 911 for an ambulance and reschedule my next patients in order to get Kate to the emergency room and admitted.

The Personal Attack

Shawn asks me to waive his latest missed appointment fee at session's end. Since I've already excused several (don't ask), I say I can't. He snorts and says all I care about is money. This is galling, of course, but arguing would send the message that I agree with his premise. Instead, I say, "If that's how you feel, you need to ask yourself why you continue to see me." Shawn snorts again and says he doesn't know what I'm talking about. This is an invitation for me to explain, and thereby run over, which I decline by saying, "Why don't you think about it, and we'll open our next session with what you come up with."

Shawn is not introspective by nature; he is a blamer. I don't expect him to bring up this exchange at the next session, and he doesn't, so I do. He tries to blow me off—"It was no big deal. I don't want to talk about it!"

"What if I want to?" I say. "Too bad, so sad, I'm out of luck?"

"Okay, okay," he rolls his eyes. "I'm sorry, okay? I shouldn't have said you're only in it for the money. I know you care." He huffs, clearly annoyed.

"I'm not bringing this up to get your apology, Shawn. This is about you keeping your word. You signed an agreement with me to pay for missed appointments. When I asked you to honor that agreement, you accused me of taking advantage of you!"

"Look, I said I was sorry, okay? Can we drop this?"

"This is important. You know not keeping your word gets you into trouble in your relationships, right? Like with your girlfriend. And your daughter. Haven't we talked about how upset they get when you tell them, say, you'll be home at 6:00 with dinner but then you don't show up until midnight, no call, no dinner?"

"Well, yeah. But that's different."

"Is it?"

And more of the same for the rest of the hour. On his way out, he grudgingly pays for the last appointment he missed.

Not charging him for the previous misses is a mistake I can't make again. Letting him off the hook has fed his baseline entitlement. As discussed in Chapter 2, Karen Horney (1950) made clear that when a person confuses a wish or a need with a claim of entitlement, that creates relationship trouble along with personal suffering. Shawn had moved from *wanting* me to waive a late fee to *expecting* me to waive it. In fact, this incident is such an iconic example of Shawn's generalized entitlement that it needs a tag. What to call it? The No Show Low Blow? Will he get it? I'll see with the next incident, for there will be another, guaranteed.

The False Emergency

Janice is a divorced mother of two boys with an irresponsible ex and a long history of obsessional worrying. At the last minute, she sobs that her job is being cut. "What am I going to do? I won't have insurance. I'll have to stop coming in. My ex is useless. I'll lose my house, and we'll be homeless." Projecting into a catastrophic future is Janice's default response to stressors.

Reframing and helping her access self-soothing and problem-solving skills are the work of the next session, so I don't go there, even though it's killing me not to. Instead, I hand her a tissue and say, "I'm so sorry. When is your last day of work?" After she answers, I say, "We'll figure it out, but not today. We have to close now. How about you come in for an extra session later this week?"

When I feel intense emotional pressure from a patient to run to the rescue and run over, I remind myself that doing so erodes trust. It's given me heart to learn that when I close as scheduled, the patient often goes on to resolve the crisis between sessions. In fact, that is exactly what Janice did. This confirms the codependent—more accurately, coregulated—nature of the pressure and the therapeutic validity of not yielding to it.

Flattery Will Get You Nowhere

Nancy's brother, aged forty, has been a source of anguish for her since their teens, when he fell into the abyss of addiction and criminal activity. "He just got out of jail and wants to stay clean," she tells me. "You're the only one who can help him!"

"That's not true," I say, "and besides, I can't provide the treatment he needs in my out-patient office."

"But he's been to all the rehabs around here and he's fooled all the other shrinks. I know *you'll* outsmart him! Please, please see him," she begs.

"Thank you for your confidence in me, but I can't. I'm sorry." She starts to plead, but I hold up my hand in the universal stop gesture. "I wish we had more time, but we have to end now." She leaves angry, and I'm afraid she won't come back. But she does.

"So . . . , we're okay?" I ask. She looks at me askance and says, "What are you talking about?" When she'd failed to make her problem mine, she'd moved on and found another solution, no hard feelings. I've learned over the years that most patients will do this when you draw firm lines. And if they don't, that merits exploration.

Therapist Blunder

The last-minute gaffe I made with my gentle, fragile, and elderly schizophrenic patient Ed (from Chapter 2)—"Come on, we both know you're crazy! That's why you're here!"—makes me cringe whenever I remember it. The resulting breach in our connection required immediate attention. Fortunately, our patient–clinician bond was strong, so communicating my remorse to Ed with whole-body expression repaired the breach quickly. If I have to run over a few minutes to make such reparations, so be it. This is one of the few situations where I believe *not* ending on time is clinically justified. Letting a patient leave injured by something I said or did is antitherapeutic, a violation of the do-no-harm mandate.

A last-minute gaffe can take as many forms as there are therapists, the one commonality being that it happens as the session is ending. Maintaining trust requires we openly acknowledge when we make mistakes and then do whatever works to repair our connection with the patient, for however many sessions that takes. If the patient remains unforgiving, that needs to be examined as well.

The Hot Seat

Bev, midfifties, is a righteous perfectionist who chronically considers divorcing her husband. Thirty years in, she has yet to make her move. Standing up to leave, she says, "By the way, your husband's car is a disgrace! Why don't you make him clean it up?"

Being married, both of us psychiatrists, and in practice together in a small town makes us (very) minor celebrities. Plus, everybody knows everybody's car. Bev has probably parked next to his in the parking lot, glanced in as she walked by, and been appalled. My darling husband uses his car as a combination waste basket and laundry hamper.

Bev's question is so layered with multiple implications and judgments—the most obvious being that I'm a bad wife and, by extension, a bad therapist—that I'm happy to be *confident* it is therapeutic to end on time. I definitely need the time between sessions to think things through. But right now, I'm on the spot. What to say? I stifle the urge to remind her, *People who live in glass houses shouldn't throw stones.* She doesn't need scolding; she needs to think. I go with, "I want to stay married?" She looks startled. *Good. Think about that.* I smile. She gives me the side eye over her shoulder on her way out.

At the next session, she makes my life easy by asking, "How can you be okay with your husband trashing his car?"

"I don't like it," I say, "but I decided long ago that his car is his business. I'm not going to ride in it, so why argue about it? Staying happily married is all about picking your battles." She looks puzzled. Has it never occurred to her to triage what she argues about with her husband? I see the way forward.

Last-minute personal questions are always interesting and have much to teach us about the patient, and ourselves. If, like me, you tend to be reactive to these kinds of emotional challenges, practice not feeling obliged to answer. To introduce a pause before speaking, one strategy I like is counting to ten (or higher) slowly in my head as I consider my response. Another excellent strategy is deflecting— "Let's talk about this next time." A third option is to answer a question enigmatically by asking one of your own, as I did with Bev. Her question, and my response, jump-started a new direction in the treatment, beginning with exploring the role of compromise in marriage and then going deeper into her past and her parent's relationship.

•

These are just a few doorknob moments I've experienced. You, of course, are sure to have your own. To engender trust, prevent stagnation, and keep the treatment thriving, make it safe for the client to drop a last-minute stunner—end on time.

> Expect the unexpected. And whenever possible, be the unexpected.
>
> — LYNDA BARRY, *Cruddy: An Illustrated Novel*

The New Triangle

You and the Patient,
Plus the "Inanimate Third"

The in vivo experiment forced upon clinicians in the United States and abroad by the COVID-19 pandemic has proven surprisingly successful. Remote work is now embedded in general therapy practice (Markowitz et al., 2021; Tajan et al., 2023) as a viable way of providing treatment, regardless of therapeutic orientation (Stadler et al., 2023).

Before the pandemic, remote work was a specialized niche intervention and used primarily as an adjunct to in-person (aka face-to-face) sessions. That changed overnight in March 2020 when the CDC mandated a national shutdown to prevent the spread of the virus. Up to that point, in our upstate New York practice, my husband and I provided in-person treatment only. We had a little experience with working by phone and none with video chat. Like everyone else, to continue "seeing" patients we had to improvise and experiment with the various options: traditional phone, cell phone apps, and internet video chat (Zoom, Doxy.me, and others).

Most of our colleagues in urban areas, where internet service tends to be reliable and patients tech savvy, preferred video chat. We, however, settled on working primarily by phone because, surprisingly, most of our patients preferred the phone. Reviewing the literature revealed this was true for other clinicians as well (Markowitz et al., 2021). Why would that be? Well, the phone is easy. All our patients have phones (traditional landlines or cell phones), know how to use them, and are able to use them even when cognitively impaired by symptoms. Obvious other reasons included not having access to the internet (common in our rural community); not owning a computer, tablet, or smartphone (also common); not having internet skills (the elderly, the tech challenged); not wanting to learn those skills; or simply being too ill to manage being online.

A less obvious reason, but possibly more compelling for some patients, was this. Patients make themselves vulnerable when they shower and dress to come to see me in the neutral space of my office. A video chat takes away that sense of safe neutrality by letting me peer into their homes—a violation of their privacy, which may arouse a variety of trust-undermining feelings, such as of shame, anxiety, and humiliation (Jessner et al., 2021; Stefan et al., 2021). "It's a mess! I don't want you to see it," one patient admitted to me.

On the other hand, video telepsychotherapy has many positives. Being able to see each other provides valuable visual feedback that enhances implicit, nonverbal communication between the patient–clinician dyad. We can take in the patient's facial expressions and body language, along with their vocal tone and prosody, and they ours. If transmission is good, and we each have the computer camera positioned at natural eye level, the virtual interaction sometimes approximates live engagement enough to enable me to not mind the device between us.

Technical problems with both options interfere to varying degrees with the intimacy our sensitive work requires. Direct eye contact is iffy during videoconferencing. Usually, you can only tell if the patient is looking at the camera or not (Ferber & Weller, 2020; Jessner et al., 2021). Distractions include the self-view in the upper right corner of the screen, and the sounds and/or sights of family members or pets in the background. The countless distortions that are a function of how video images are digitally encoded, decoded, and adjusted cause the image frequently to freeze, blur, or drop, or worst of all, to be out of sync with the audio. Bad weather—a frequent occurrence where we live—only makes this worse. These glitches and delays scramble subtle social cues and interfere with perceptual processing.

The phone deprives us of visual cues, but that absence sharpens hearing and increases sensitivity to subtle nuances of speech rate, rhythm, tone, and—this was really helpful—the client's breathing (Gitlin, 2020; Jessner et al., 2021). The rate of speech transmission is closer to in-person conversation, and the fidelity of sound can be higher, especially from a landline, which is what I use when calling patients.

Therapeutic interaction—mutual understanding—is fundamentally grounded in implicit and nonverbal communication (Jessner et al., 2021; Stadler et al., 2023), which is reduced in telepsychotherapy. Maintaining a consistent intimate focus requires more intense and prolonged concentration than in-person work. Understanding silence, for example, is difficult in remote work. Is the silence active because the patient is thinking, or it is a disturbance in the connection (Jessner et al., 2021)? "A pause can mean [too] many things" (Markowitz et al., 2021, p. 8). The lack of perceptual, sensory data forces us to rely heavily on verbal feedback from patients. "This places a high demand on patients to put their perception into words. Patients are extraordinarily challenged in verbalizing their emotions" (Stadler et al., 2023, p. 16).

Unceasingly, out of consciousness, these challenges attend each telepsychotherapy session—phone or video chat—and I strained to fill in the gaps. Even a short workday of only telepsychotherapy left me spent as if I'd been up all night on call—sand in my eyes, physically sore, running on fumes. Rather than feeling connected, I sometimes felt the opposite: anxious, isolated, and distanced. Regardless of which remote option we prefer, "we all find remote psychotherapy physically and psychically more exhausting than the in-person variety" (Markowitz et al., 2021, p. 8).

And yet, despite these demands, I've been delighted to experience many moments in session when my available senses are fully engaged, as are the patient's. That sense of powerful connection between us makes me forget, temporarily, that our connection is mediated by an electronic device (Ferber & Weller, 2020; Jessner et al., 2021). It has been thrilling—and rejuvenating—to find myself doing deep, transformational work with patients despite the loss of many perceptual cues and technical limitations (Gitlin, 2020).

Ferber and Weller (2020)'s fascinating paper asks two critical questions: Can remote therapy be curative? Does the electronic device used to manage sessions unite or separate therapist and patient? They coined the term "inanimate third" to discuss the objective electronic device in the therapeutic process in contrast to the subjective emotional processes of patient and clinician. They suggested the term "social paradox" to describe how the phone and/or computer symbolizes both distance and intimacy, as well as separation and unity, in the treatment relationship.

> To perform effective treatment online one needs to maintain a sense of presence. This is a neurological state. . . . Online presence is a state termed "telepresence." Telepresence is an experience of the state of presence where awareness of the mediating device temporarily recedes or disappears. (p. 2)

Thus, virtual reality is real, though different from actual reality. The authors explain that the patient's experience of real emotional progression virtually is the result of embodiment, because bodily sensations encode social reality. Bodily experiences encode *any* social reality, be it actual, virtual, film, or paperback fiction. Have you ever found yourself lovingly stroking the cover of an engrossing novel you've just finished? While immersed in the reading experience, the fictional characters become our social reality. Turning the last page ends that connection. Stroking the cover embodies and expresses a rich mix of feelings, including love and loss.

Mirror neurons in the brain establish a perception of the other person on the screen of our mind when we are doing something together. Mirror neurons fire not only when we do something but when we watch others doing it too (McGilchrist, 2009). This is why your kid watches his friend playing a video game with as much interest as if he were playing it himself. Mirror neurons are behind why, when we imitate something we are watching, that approximates directly experiencing it.

But it goes further than this. Mental representation, in the absence of direct visual or other stimulus—in other words, imagining—brings into play some of the same neurons that are involved in direct perception. . . . Imagining something, watching someone else do something, and doing it ourselves share important neural foundations. (p. 250)

Ferber and Weller (2020) suggest this perceptual process coincides with "reverie, reflection, and emotional meeting between patient and therapist within their shared fantasies and experience of the analytic third" (p. 2). While sensory input is altered when using the telephone or screen, the output or embodiment still exists. "Embodiment of the patient and therapist in their respective imaginations may turn the electronic device, the inanimate third, alive" (p. 2). I understand this to mean the sense in which a child experiences her stuffed doggy as alive. She knows it isn't really, but it lives in her mind as if it were.

Following the intersubjective school of psychoanalysis, Ferber and Weller (2020) maintain that both an in-person and a virtual encounter require therapist and patient to maintain the same level of availability for reverie. This allows for a mutual coregulation of affects and facilitates dialogue composed of interaction cycles. Content is less important than the "progression of the dialogue, the creation of mutual perceptions of self and other, and its aligned emotion regulation" (p. 6). Accuracy of perception can be curative. Therapists use the patient's verbal content, both manifest and latent, to express how they perceive the patient, "thus fulfilling the deepest wish of any patient: which is to be understood" (p. 7).

Feeling better is what counts in psychotherapy and I can tell even through the phone when a patient's mood lifts. In fact, when the phones go down or cell calls drop, my mind and the patient's continue living in the past, present, and future, unlimited by the device's presence or absence. Once we reconnect and after we briefly process the upset caused by device failure, most patients are able to recapture their train of thought and move forward from the point of interruption. The mind can toggle between allowing the device to recede to "uncanny" and back to "inanimate" as required. Synchronous dialogue (connecting in live time) facilitated by the inanimate third makes emotional engagement possible from a distance. Our minds are not dependent on location to connect (Ferber & Weller, 2020).

The term "social paradox" manifests in the experience of telepresence, where deep work can be done, and in the breaking of telepresence, where distance and device intrude through technical problems, leaving therapist and patient stranded in their respective spaces, alone. The paradox of a relationship containing both—distance in two environments and embodied closeness in a shared conscious and unconscious space—needs to be held in the mind, experienced, and (eventually) explored. Ferber and Weller (2020) optimistically conclude that "containment by therapeutic dialogue is possible as the existence of the dialogue eliminates elements of the paradox" (p. 1).

What about doorknob moments? Do they happen in telepsychotherapy? Of course they do. Are they any different coming through the screen or phone than face to face? Not really. The two defining characteristics of doorknob moments are, one, their unexpected appearance just as the session is ending, which, two, reveals the patient's trust in us, and in the therapeutic process. Thus, a doorknob moment reflects the deep nature of the work being done, whether by telepsychotherapy or in person. Whether you are working face to face or remotely, if you've educated the patient ahead of time that doorknob moments happen unexpectedly, it's much easier to deftly end on time.

You may recall my trauma patient Sarah that I described at the beginning of this book. Like many PTSD patients, she found it easier to reveal and process her horrific past by phone than in person (Bongaerts et al., 2022; Stadler et al., 2023). She said she felt safer being at home than with me at the office, and not being able to see me decreased her level of shame when sharing her past. She said hearing my voice was more than enough. The lack of perceptual sensory data—not seeing my face, not reading my body language—worked for her. For me, the loss of perceptual sensory data—scanning her face and eyes, reading her body language, tracking affective nuance—was difficult but still manageable.

We'd been working by phone for many months when she dropped the following shocker.

> Just as I started to say our time was up, Sarah told me when she was fourteen, she was sexually molested for months by the sixteen-year-old son of the foster family she'd been placed with. "He knocked me up. I ran away on a Greyhound bus and found a hospital," she sobbed into my ear. "I got an abortion. I had to," she wailed. "What else could I do?" She wept harder. "I'm going to hell, I know it."
>
> I was speechless. *Fourteen.* She escaped. Got herself to a hospital. She survived. Now in her forties, Sarah wept the bitter, unwilling tears of the tormented. Like many survivors of childhood sexual and physical abuse, she despised herself for the terror

and rage she'd felt back then, and now, as always when she broke down, she was crushed with shame for crying uncontrollably (van der Kolk, 2014, p. 13).

I looked at the clock on the end table. I had fifteen minutes before my next patient. This wasn't the first doorknob moment Sarah and I had weathered together. I knew she was struggling to pull herself together. Did she drop this bombshell counting on me to end on time? Most likely. Did she know she was going to fall apart in the telling? Hardly.

I didn't extend the session to help her process what she'd just revealed. Instead, I used those extra minutes to help her regain control of herself. "Sarah, we need to wrap up. Do you have tissues handy?"

I heard rustles as she moved in her chair, heavy breathing, wet sniffles. "Uh, no."

"Go ahead and get some."

"Okay." There was the white-noise *clunk* of the phone dropped on wood. . . . Silence. . . . Muffled honks as she blew her nose a few times. "Okay," she said thickly into my ear. "I'm okay."

"Good," I said. "How about we pick this up next time?"

"Okay," she said, sounding more herself.

"Any last words?" I asked.

"I'm so tired. I'm going to take a nap."

"Sounds good. Rest easy. We'll talk next week."

"Thanks." I needed a nap too, but alas, I had miles to go.

Closing had taken about ten minutes. My aim always is to hold the deadline, but an aim isn't a hard rule. Running over a few minutes to end gently doesn't break the overall pattern of consistency, reliability, and trust that we work so hard to maintain—provided, of course, that we don't address the new material beyond saying we'll deal with it together in future.

If we had been meeting face to face, Sarah might have used her travel time home to decompress, and the time before the next session to reflect on what she wanted to bring up. In many studies (Stadler et al., 2023; Stefan et al., 2021; Stoll et al., 2019; Thase et al., 2020; Weightman, 2020), travel has been presented as a burden in terms of cost and time. But, interestingly, a few studies (Galasinski et al., 2022; Jessner et al., 2021; Markowitz et al., 2021) have reported that patients find their traveling time special and meaningful. Travel to and from therapy appears to be spent actively—it is time to review past sessions before the current one, and time to process the current one afterward. The physical journey becomes a rite of passage, a culturally sanctioned transition from one state to another, between nontherapy time and therapy time. Travel time thus has meaning beyond simple movement in time and space—it is part of the process of change. During the pandemic, patients did not replace this meaningful time with other actions, such as a walk or meditation, and experienced not being able to travel to and from sessions as a loss (Galasinski et al., 2022).

Many studies assert that remote work is as effective as in-person sessions (Bandelow & Wedekind, 2022; Basile et al., 2022; Datta et al., 2022; Lamb et al., 2019; Markowitz et al., 2021; Matsumoto et al., 2021; Probst et al., 2021; Shanley & Reddi, 2022; Shatri et al., 2021; Tajan et al., 2023; Thase et al., 2020; Wright & Caudill, 2020), including the maintenance of therapeutic alliance and empathy (Ferber & Weller, 2020; Stefan et al., 2021). Yet the literature also reveals that therapists and clinicians persist in reporting that remote work is not truly comparable to in-person work (Ferber & Weller, 2020; Humer et al., 2020; Jessner et al., 2021; Markowitz et al., 2021; Notermans & Philippot, 2022 Probst et al., 2021; Stadler et al., 2023; Stefan et al., 2021; Winter et al., 2023). That is my experience, too, as perhaps it is for you. However, out of necessity "there seems to be no question that patient access to clinicians is better than no access, and telephone or video therapy seems undoubtedly preferable to more detached media such as texting for human encounter" (Markowitz et al., 2021, p. 2).

I remain uncomfortable doing intakes and treating high-risk patients remotely. The lack of sensory perceptual data increases the odds of a misdiagnosis, and thus subsequent mistreatment. Given that I prescribe, and that diagnosis dictates medication options, that's a risk I prefer to avoid. There is little research on the use of telepsychotherapy for the treatment of psychosis, severe trauma, cognitive impairments, children, families and couples, and group therapy. What there is suggests that these types of therapy may be less suited to remote work (Tajan et al., 2023), though one study found virtual telepsychotherapy acceptable for treatment of couples and families (de Boer et al., 2021). Teenagers and young adults are the one group that benefits robustly from all forms of telepsychotherapy (Jessner et al., 2021; Rogowska, 2022), although this is also the group most vulnerable to internet misuse and addiction (Stoll et al., 2019).

And yet, what a pleasant surprise it is to be able to provide meaningful service mediated by the inanimate other. Having returned to face-to-face work, I'm finding a mix of in-person and telepsychotherapy appointments wonderfully flexible. When a patient is homebound after a knee replacement or can't come in because of a sick child or because a snowstorm makes driving the hour to my office unsafe, it is a boon to be able to meet remotely, despite the technical and sensory limitations. That remote work approximates the effectiveness of face-to-face sessions is one paradoxical gain of the pandemic. Another is that Medicare and private health insurers discontinued their arbitrary refusal to reimburse clinicians for remote work by phone and video chat. Fingers crossed that continues.

Engaging patients in transformational work via telepsychotherapy is a matter of staying alert and noticing when *all* our available senses are fully engaged, for that is when the patient's will be too. That sense of powerful connection—telepresence—helps both of us willingly suspend awareness of the electronic device in the same way an immersive movie or novel encourages us to suspend disbelief in its fiction so as to experience the journey it delivers.

There I sit in session via telepsychotherapy. Just as I am reveling in how well things are going and how alive the interaction feels, my eye lands on the clock on the side table: time to wrap up. But I don't get

> the chance—thunder claps, lightning strikes, and my
> patient rains tears. Little hairs rise to attention all over
> my body in an electrical wave.

Doorknob bombshells always come as a shock, perhaps because they are so randomly intermittent. Feeling confident that ending on time *is* therapeutic helps dissipate the jolt. Not feeling obliged to process an upsetting disclosure on the fly is one less task to manage. In my experience, closing in the wake of doorknob moments generally takes around five minutes. Sometimes, the patient gives me a second gift by delivering their revelation a few minutes before the formal end of the session, with time to wrap up. What is the first gift, you might ask? The revelation itself—new material, no matter how disturbing, prevents treatment stagnation.

If you work in a clinic, discourage the manager from scheduling your patients back to back, whether remote or in person. Ten to fifteen minutes between appointments gives you a few extra minutes to close sensitively when (not if) a patient ends on a cliff-hanger, and a few minutes for yourself afterward to clear your head. A few slow, deep breaths in and out, and you'll be ready for your next patient, and your next adventure.

ACKNOWLEDGMENTS

My heartfelt gratitude to the following people for making this book possible. I am a very fortunate woman.

Deborah Malmud, vice president, W. W. Norton, for inviting me to write this book after reading the short piece in the *Psychiatric Times* (Gitlin, 2022) on the subject, and for stellar developmental editing, which made writing it so much easier than I expected. Mariah Eppes, Sara McBride Tuohy, and the entire Norton team for being such a pleasure to work with. Special thanks to artist Lauren Graessle for the beautiful cover.

Livia Kent, editor in chief, *The Psychotherapy Networker*, for publishing my first doorknob moment article (Gitlin, 2018), thereby launching the chain of events that culminated in this book.

Jill M. Tarabula Daby, MLS, AHIP, regional medical librarian at the University of Vermont Health Network, Champlain Valley Physicians Hospital, for invaluable assistance researching the literature.

Suzette Martinez Standring, dear friend and writing buddy; for the fun, for the writing retreats during which we got so much work done, and for being this book's first reader.

Alvin Pam, PhD, and Susan Kemker, MD, for enduring friendship, mentoring, and the best kind of shop talk.

The National Society of Newspaper Columnists' Zoom Writing Space, where writers gather twice weekly to work together in silence.

Terry Boyarsky, Elle Berger, Amy Guglielmo, Kristin Kimball, Joan Janson, Kayla Forkey, Cynthia Lacki, Chris Allen, Anna Blitz, Regan Torney: for always having my writing back.

Kevin, for everything.

REFERENCES

Arlow, J. A. (1986). "Psychoanalysis and time." *Journal of the American Psychanalytic Association, 34,* 507–528.

Arnd-Caddigan, M. (2013). "Don't let the doorknob hit you: A relational-intersubjective exploration of leaving and remaining within the therapeutic frame." *Psychoanalytic Social Work, 20,* 134–149.

Arnheim, R. (1969). *Visual thinking.* University of California Press.

Bandelow, B., & Wedekind, D. (2022)."Internet psychotherapeutic interventions for anxiety disorders—a critical evaluation." *BMC Psychiatry, 22,* 441.

Barnard, M. (1986). *Sappho: A new translation.* University of California Press.

Barrett, L. F. (2020). *Seven and one-half lessons about the brain.* Houghton Mifflin Harcourt.

Barry, L. (1999). *Cruddy: An illustrated novel.* Simon and Schuster.

Barry, L. (2008). *What it is.* Drawn and Quarterly.

Barry, L. (2014). *Syllabus: Notes from an accidental professor.* Drawn and Quarterly.

Basile, V. T., Newton-John, T., & Wootton, B. M. (2022, December). "Remote cognitive-behavioral therapy for generalized anxiety disorder: A preliminary meta-analysis." *Journal of Clinical Psychology, 78*(12), 2381–2395.

Blake, W. (1977). *The portable William Blake.* Penguin Classics.

Bongaerts, H., Voorendonk, E. M., van Minnen, A., Rozendaal, L., Telkamp, B. S. D., & de Jongh, A. (2022). "Fully remote intensive trauma-focused treatment for PTSD and complex PTSD." *European Journal of Psychotraumatology, 13*(2), 2103287.

Brody, S. (2009). "On the edge: Exploring the end of the analytic hour." *Psychoanalytic Dialogues, 19,* 87–97.

Cohen-Sheehy, B. I., Delgrazan, A. I., Reagh, Z. M., Crivelli-Decker, J. E., Kim, K., Barnett, A. J., Zacks, J. M., & Ranganath, C. (2021). "The hippocampus constructs narrative memories across distant events." *Current Biology, 31*(22), 4935–4945.

Cozolino, L. (2021). *The development of a therapist: Healing others–healing self.* Norton.

Csikszentmihaly, M. (2008). *Flow: The psychology of optimum experience.* Harper Perennial.

Datta, R., Vishwanath, R., & Shenoy, S. (2022). "Are remote psychotherapy/remediation efforts accessible and feasible in patients with schizophrenia? A narrative review." *Egyptian Journal of Neurology, Psychiatry and Neurosurgery, 58*(1), 136.

de Boer, K., Muir, S. D., Silva, S. S. M., Nedelijkovic, M., Seabrook, E., Thomas, N., & Meyer, D. (2021, April). "Videoconferencing psychotherapy for couples and families: A systematic review." *Journal of Marital and Family Therapy, 47*(2), 259–288.

Faden, J., & Gorton, G. (2018). "The doorknob phenomenon in clinical practice." *American Family Physician,* *98*(1), 52–53.

Ferber, S. G., & Weller, A. (2020, May). "The inanimate third: Going beyond psychodynamic approaches for remote psychotherapy during the COVID-19 pandemic." *British Journal of Psychotherapy, 38*(2), 316–337.

Fromm, E. (1998). *The Art of Listening.* Continuum.

Gabbard, G. O. (1982). "The exit line: Heightened transference-countertransference manifestations at the end of the hour." *Journal of the American Psychoanalytic Association, 30*(3), 579–598.

Galasinski, D., Ziotkowska, J., & Witkowicz, M. (2022). "Experience of the absence of the journey to sessions in clients' narratives about online psychotherapy." *Frontiers in Psychology, 13,* 798960.

Gans, J. S. (2016). "'Our time is up': A relational perspective on the ending of a single psychotherapy session." *American Journal of Psychotherapy, 70*(4), 413–427.

Gitlin, D. V. (2018, September-October). "Doorknob moments: Handling end-of-session bombshells." *The Psychotherapy Networker,* 17–18.

Gitlin, D. V. (2019, February 7). "Managing confidentiality: Three things I learned from my small-town practice." *The Psychotherapy Networker.* https://www.psych otherapynetworker.org/post/managing-confidentiality -three-things-i-learned-from-my-small-town-practice

Gitlin, D. V. (2020, November–December). "The surprising intimacy of phone sessions." *Psychotherapy Networker,* 26–27.

Gitlin, D. V. (2022, January). "Doorknob moments: Why they happen and how to use them." *Psychiatric Times*, 24–25.

Gutheil, T. G., & Simon, R. I. (1995). "Between the chair and the door: Boundary issues in the therapeutic 'transition zone.'" *Harvard Review of Psychiatry*, 2(6), 336–340.

Hartocollis, P. (2003). "Time and the psychoanalytic situation." *Psychoanalytic Quarterly*, 72, 939–957. https://doi.org/10.1002/j.2167-4086.2003.tb00145.x

Horney, K. (1950). *Neurosis and human growth: The struggle toward self-realization.* Norton.

Humer, E., Stippi, P., Pieh, C., Pryss, R., & Probst, T. (2020, November 27). "Experiences of psychotherapists with remote psychotherapy during the COVID-19 pandemic: Cross-sectional Web-based survey study." *Journal of Medical Internet Research*, 22(11), e20246. https://doi.org/10.2196/20246

Jackson, G. (2005). "'Oh . . . by the way . . . ': Doorknob syndrome." *Journal of Clinical Practice*, 59(8), 869.

Jessner, A., Muckenhuber, J., & Lunglmayr, B. (2021). "Psychodynamic therapists' subjective experiences with remote psychotherapy during the COVID-19 pandemic—a qualitative study with therapists practicing guided affective imagery, hypnosis, and autogenous relaxation." *Frontiers in Psychology*, 12, 777102.

Kent, C., & Steward, J. (2008). "Ten rules for students, teachers and life." In *Learning by heart: Teachings to free the creative spirit.* Allworth.

King, S. (2000). *On Writing: A Memoir of the Craft.* Scribner.

Kowalski, C. P., McQuillan, D. B., Chawla, N., Lyles, C.,

Altschuler, A., Uratsu, C. S., Bayliss, E. A., Heisler, M., & Grant, R. W. (2018). "'The hand on the doorknob': Visit agenda setting by complex patients and their primary care physicians." *Journal of the American Board of Family Medicine, 31*(1), 29–37. https://www.jabfm.org/content/31/1/29

Lamb, T., Pachana, N. A., & Dissanayaka, N. (2019, August). "Update of recent literature on remotely delivered psychotherapy interventions for anxiety and depression." *Telemedicine Journal and e-Health, 25*(8), 671–677.

Langs, R. (1984). "Making interpretations and securing the frame: Sources of danger for psychotherapists." *International Journal of Psychoanalytic Psychotherapy, 10,* 3–23.

Markowitz, J. C., Milrod, B., Heckman, T. G., Bergman, M., Amsalem, D., Zalman, H., Ballas, T., & Neria, Y. (2021, March 1). "Psychotherapy at a distance." *American Journal of Psychiatry, 178*(3), 240–246. https://ajp.psychiatryonline.org/doi/10.1176/appi.ajp.2020.20050557

Matsumoto, K., Hamatani, S., & Shimizu, E. (2021, December 13). "Effectiveness of videoconference-delivered cognitive behavioral therapy for adults with psychiatric disorders: Systematic and meta-analytic review." *Journal of Medical Internet Research, 23*(12), e31293.

McGilchrist, I. (2009). *The master and his emissary: The divided brain and the making of the Western world.* Yale University Press.

Notermans, J., & Philippot, P. (2022, September). "Psychotherapy under lockdown: The use and experience of teleconsultation by psychotherapists during the first wave of the COVID-19 pandemic." *Clinical Psychology in Europe*, *4*(3), e6821.

Patchett, A. (2013). *This is the story of a happy marriage*. Harper Perennial.

Poetry Foundation. (n.d.). "Robert Frost." https://www.poetryfoundation.org/poets/robert-frost

Probst, T., Haid, B., Schimbock, W., Reisinger, A., Gasser, M., Eichberger-Heckmann, H., Stippl, P., Jesser, A., Humer, E., Korecka, N., & Pieh, C. (2021, July–August). "Therapeutic interventions in in-person and remote psychotherapy: Survey with psychotherapists and patients experiencing in-person and remote psychotherapy during COVID-19." *Clinical Psychology and Psychotherapy*, *28*(4), 988–1000.

Rogowska, A. (2022, November). "Remote interventions to support students' psychological well-being during the COVID-19 pandemic: A narrative review of recent approaches." *International Journal of Environmental Research and Public Health*, *19*(21), 14040.

Schore, A. N. (2019). *Right brain psychotherapy*. Norton.

Shanley, I., Jones, C., & Reddi, N. (2022, May). "Medical psychotherapy training and COVID-19 pandemic." *British Journal of Psychotherapy*, *38*(2), 338–352.

Shatri, H., Prabu, O. G., Tetrasiwi, E. N., Faisal, E., Putranto, R., & Ismail, R. I. (2021). "The role of online psychotherapy in COVID-19: An evidence based clinical review." *Acta Medica Indonesiana*, *53*(3), 352–359.

Siegel, D. J. (2012). *Pocket guide to interpersonal neurobiology: An integrative handbook of the mind*. Norton.

Sperry, R. W. (1961). "Cerebral Organization and Behavior: The split brain behaves in many respects like two separate brains, providing new research possibilities." *Science. 133*(3466): 1749–1757.

Sperry, R. W. (1974). *Classic experiments in psychology.* Greenwood Press.

Stadler, M., Jesser, A., Humer, E., Haid, B., Stippl, P., Schimbock, W., Maab, E., Schwanzar, H., Leithner, D., Pieh, C., & Probst, T. (2023, February). "Remote psychotherapy during the COVID-19 pandemic: A mixed-methods study on the changes experienced by Austrian psychotherapists." *Life (Basel), 13*(2), 360.

Stefan, R., Manti, G., Hofner, C., Stammer, J., Hochgerner, M., & Petersdorfer, K. (2021). "Remote psychotherapy during the COVID-19 pandemic: Experiences with the transition and the therapeutic relationship. a longitudinal mixed-methods study." *Frontiers in Psychology, 12*, 743430.

Stoll, J., Muller, J. A., & Trachsel, M. (2019). "Ethical issues in online psychotherapy: A narrative review." *Frontiers in Psychiatry, 10*, 993.

Stout, M. (2006). *The sociopath next door.* Harmony.

Sullivan, H. S. (1953). *The interpersonal theory of psychiatry.* Norton.

Tajan, N., Deves, M., & Potier, R. (2023). "Tele-psychotherapy during the COVID-19 pandemic: A mini-review." *Frontiers in Psychiatry, 14*, 1060961.

Tharp, T. (2003). *The creative habit: Learn it and use it for life.* Simon and Shuster.

Thase, M. E., McCrone, P., Barrett, M. S., Eells, T. D., Wisniewski, S. R., Balasubramani, G. K., Brown, G. K., & Wright, J. H. (2020, May). "Improving cost-effectiveness and access to cognitive behavior therapy for depression: Proving remote-ready, computer-assisted psychotherapy in times of crisis and beyond." *Psychotherapy and Psychosomatics*, *89*(5), 307–313.

van der Kolk, B. (2014). *The body keeps the score: Brain, mind, and body in the healing of trauma*. Penguin Books.

Waugaman, R. M. (1992). "Analytic time." *The Journal of the American Psychoanalytic Association*, *20*(1), 29–47.

Weightman, M. (2020, June). "Digital psychotherapy as an effective and timely treatment option for depression and anxiety disorders: Implications for rural and remote practice." *Journal of International Medical Research*, *48*(6), 0300060520928686.

Westlake, D. (1974). *Jimmy the kid*. Mysterious Press.

Wiggins, K. M. (1983). "The patient's relation to time during the final minutes of a psychotherapy session." *American Journal of Psychotherapy*, *37*(1), 62–68.

Winnicott, D. W. (1947). *The child, the family, and the outside world*. Penguin Books.

Winter, S., Jesser, A., Probst, T., Schaffler, Y., Kisler, I., Haid, B., Pieh, C., & Humer, E. (2023). "How the COVID-19 pandemic affects the provision of psychotherapy: Results from three online surveys on Austrian psychotherapists." *International Journal of Environmental Research and Public Health*, *20*(3), 1961.

Wittink, M. N., Walsh, P., Yilmaz, S., Mendoza, M., Street,

R. L., Jr., Chapman, B. P., & Duberstein, P. (2018). "Patient priorities and the doorknob phenomenon in primary care: Can technology improve disclosure of patient stressors?" *Patient Education and Counseling, 101*(2), 214–220.

Wright, J. H., & Caudill, R. (2020, March 26). "Remote treatment delivery in response to the COVID-19 pandemic." *Psychotherapy and Psychosomatics, 89*(3), 1–3.

Yalom, I. (2002). *The gift of therapy: An open letter to a new generation of therapists and their patients.* Harper Perennial.

Yalom, I. D., and Elkin, G. (1991). *Every day gets a little closer: A twice-told therapy.* Basic Books.

Zinsser, W. (2009, December 1) "Writing English as a second language." *The American Scholar,* https://theamericanscholar.org/writing-english-as-a-second-language/

INDEX

ABOUT THE AUTHOR

Daniela V. Gitlin, MD has been a psychiatrist in private practice for over thirty years. In addition to taking care of patients, running the practice, and staying married, she writes for *The Psychotherapy Networker* and blogs at danielagitlin.com. Her memoir, *Practice, Practice, Practice: This Psychiatrist's Life*, spans twenty-five years of treatment mishaps, patient ambushes, and clinician pratfalls, and affirms that flawless performance is not required for a therapist to be genuinely helpful. It was selected a finalist by the 2021 International Book Awards.